THE DOG WALKER'S GUIDE TO GOD

THE
DOG
WALKER'S
GUIDE TO
GOD

52 musings on companionship,
Divine and human

HENRY MARTIN

DARTON·LONGMAN+TODD

First published in 2023 by
Darton, Longman and Todd Ltd
1 Spencer Court
140 – 142 Wandsworth High Street
London SW18 4JJ

ISBN: 978-1-915412-02-7

A catalogue record for this book is available from the British Library.

Printed and bound in Great Britain by Bell & Bain, Glasgow

FOR HAYDN

CONTENTS

INTRODUCTION

'Consider the dog, trotting along, beside you …'

Why not? Jesus invites us to, 'Consider the lilies of the field …' and 'Consider the birds of the air …'.

So how about, 'Consider the dog, sleeping at your feet?'

The argument runs like this: Lilies? if God gives such temporary plants such astonishing arraignment, how much more will God clothe us, his beloved humans! Birds? if God feeds them, though they neither farm nor store, how much more will God feed us!

And dogs? Can they, like lilies and birds, teach us about God? Are there lessons along the same lines: a dog related observation, followed by the question, 'And how much more will God …'?

The technical term for this thought process is '*qal wahomer*' (literally, 'light and heavy') and Rabbi Hillel made it one of his seven rules of biblical interpretation. The basic pattern is simple: '*if this small thing is true, then how much more will this much bigger thing also be true?*' We find it in the Psalms. When we read, 'The Lord is my shepherd, I shall not want' we are fully expected to make the jump, 'Well if that is how it is with sheep and shepherds, *how much more so* is it with us and God!' Jesus also used '*qal wahomer*':

'Suppose one of you has only one sheep and it falls into a pit on the sabbath; will you not lay hold of it and lift it out? How much more valuable is a human being than a sheep!'[1]

and,

'If you then, who are evil, know how to give good gifts to your children, how much more will your Father in heaven give good things to those who ask him!'[2]

Does it work with our dogs too? This book hopes so and often asks, 'If something is so with us and our dogs, *how much more* might it be so with God and us!' There are fifty-two short readings, each offering a few minutes of inspiration before taking the dog out and then a thought to be chewed, as you go.

'*Qal wahomer*' cannot be applied in every situation. I cannot say, 'If I think this politician is an idiot, *how much more* does God despise him!' or, 'If I want a new car, *how much more* does God want me to have a Ferrari!' Christians should only use '*Qal wahomer*' when the initial small thing is consistent with God as revealed by Jesus of Nazareth, otherwise the entire process fails. The fruits of God's Spirit are another possible measure. If our starting point is at odds with any of the following: love, joy, peace, patience, kindness, generosity, faithfulness, gentleness, and self-control,[3] then simply enlarging it will not make it true of God.

Hopefully this book will be useful for those who are housebound, and possibly even for those not lucky enough to have a dog currently in their lives, since its themes are universal. Having said that, it was dreamt up on dog walks and probably best explored by those with that blessed combination: a curiosity about God *and* a canine companion trotting alongside.

---

[1]   Matthew 12:11-12.
[2]   Matthew 7:11.
[3]   Galatians 5:22-23.

PART 1

SOME BIG DIFFERENCES BETWEEN HUMANS AND DOGS AND GOD

1

DO YOU SEE
WHAT I SEE?

Sometimes I stop in my tracks, arrested by beauty. One morning it was the rising sun, caught in a thousand sunflower petals. 'Just look at that'. I said to the dog, 'isn't it wonderful?' The dog seemed nonplussed at this interruption to his walk. So I asked, 'Aren't you interested? What's wrong with you?' Shortly after we had resumed, he lurched off, yanking my arm and almost causing me to fall. Now it was my turn to feel unimpressed. He did not notice. He had fallen fully for a scent that demanded further investigation. If he could speak, he might have said to me, 'Just smell that. Isn't it intriguing? You don't get it? What's wrong with you?'

How we receive information marks a major difference between us and our dogs. Human brains have evolved to favour seeing over all other methods of perception. Those of us fortunate to be sighted rely very heavily on this one sense. It takes over our language. We say, 'I *see*' rather than, 'I understand' and we have points of *view*. We maintain that seeing is believing. If we are deceived we complain that the wool has been pulled over *our eyes*.

13

Dogs are different. They depend less on sight and more on scent, recognising a range of smells far beyond human imagining. Had the risen Jesus appeared to dogs, he might have said to the one that doubted, not, 'Blessed are those, who did not see and yet still believed', but rather, 'Blessed are those, who did not catch my scent and yet still believed.' This canine-human mismatch in perception goes a long way in explaining certain disconnections as we and our dogs walk together.

The following analogy helps: a postage stamp, stuck onto A4 paper represents the range of the human nose. In contrast, a dog's range is more like the whole sheet of A4. When we respect dogs' superiority in the sniffing game, we start to explore new possibilities. We have long known that dogs can detect buried truffles and hidden drugs but it now appears that they can alert us to undiagnosed cancers and asymptomatic coronavirus carriers. The key here is accepting that dogs have a skill beyond human understanding.

If our perception is different from dogs, how much more is God's perception different from ours? As the designer of both the human eye and the canine nose, God receives the full scope of available information. If a dog's nose confronts us with our limitations, could we not apply the same thinking to God, only more so? There are dimensions to reality beyond both human and canine knowing. God alone misses nothing by scent or sight or by any other sense. The key here is accepting that God exists within *and* beyond the realms of our perception, and our wisest approach is surely humility.

 Something to chew as your dog walks alongside you
What might God 'see' that we do not?

SO JUST TO RECAP BRIEFLY, AS WE'VE BEEN THROUGHT THIS SEVERAL TIMES BEFORE...

2

IF I COULD TALK TO
THE ANIMALS...

'I'm only keeping you on this lead because you have this habit of running away and then not coming back. Can you understand that?'

I can only guess how daft I sound as I say this, standing in the drizzle on a path, looking down a taut lead at a dog whose attention is firmly fixed on a rustle in the undergrowth. Nevertheless I continue with my lecture, 'And when you lurch like that, it's entirely counterproductive; it hurts me, presumably it's uncomfortable for you and ultimately, it gets you nowhere. You're never going to catch that hare.'

Quite possibly this talking does nothing at all for the dog; my words being just another background noise that fails to penetrate 'the Zone' he has entered. But I persist, placing more trust in my tone than in my actual words, as I try to bring the dog down, back to a calmer, more receptive place.

Some friends have an older dog. Ayla is a no-nonsense dame: a gentle, attentive spaniel who maintains her boundaries very clearly, especially when confronted by younger, friskier dogs. She is a good tutor. She sets a good example, modelling the kind of cooperation humans require. I enjoy our walks together, believing that as we go, she is passing on, in ways far beyond human comprehension, the wisdom of her many years to our sometimes over-bouncy teenager.

When she's not around and I am struggling to get through to our dog, I find myself wishing I could become a dog - for just five minutes. And as a fellow dog, I would be able to communicate directly dog to dog. Our recently rescued mutt would completely 'get' my meaning and learn a happier way to co-exist with us. I'd be able to keep him safe from himself, because he would understand me whenever I said things like, 'You see the horns on the mother of that calf you're eyeing up? Well they're not for decoration!'

Would five minutes be enough though? Now that I think about it, I'd need more time to get used to my new body and to learn how to 'talk' dog fluently. Ideally, I would start off as a pup, grow up living an authentic dog life and thus naturally acquire all the skills necessary for communicating my wisdom. Of course, I'm now veering towards some version of the Incarnation – an 'in-canine-ation'? (maybe not). Leaving word-play aside, I remember that, as fully human, born of a woman, learning and growing as one of us, Jesus communicated with us in ways that God had, up to then, not managed. But even with such a radical approach, Jesus could not get through to everyone. He stood face to face with us. His message was entirely for our own good. But some remained wilfully locked in their preferred 'zone'. Usually these were fearful people who saw only what they had to lose. However, those who did listen found a much better way of co-existing, not just with God but also with each other.

Of course there is no way for me to become a dog, so I will continue to stand in the drizzle, explaining and reasoning as if my dog appreciates my logic. Over time a few things seem to be sinking in. Maybe he understands more than he's letting on.

Something to chew as your dog walks alongside you
What one thing would I like to get through to my dog? And what one thing does God want to get through to me?

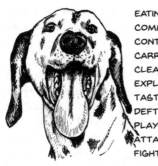

EATING
COMMUNICATING
CONTROLLING TEMPERATURE
CARRYING
CLEANING
EXPLORING
TASTING
DEFT HANDLING
PLAYING
ATTACKING
FIGHTING

3

THE AMAZING MULTI-TOOL

A dog's mouth is an incredible device. Consider its soft mobility, which can hold an egg without cracking its shell. It is a wondrous, multifunctioning apparatus designed not only to consume, communicate and control body temperature (which is why dogs pant so much when hot) but also to carry, clean and explore. In short, any task that requires deft handling, a dog accomplishes with its mouth. Rough work is also mouth business. A dog's main weapons are all loaded in its mouth; its claws do not rip and tear as felines' do, a dog relies on its teeth. There's a crude expression of extreme appreciation, we say 'That's the dog's ...' ... well, think about the opposite extremity ... which is bizarre because what's truly impressive about a dog is its mouth.

Human beings are also wonderfully made, but our evolution has taken us on a different path. Many of our pre-human ancestors' mouth-tasks have been reassigned to our front paws, which developed significantly when freed from weight-bearing duties, as we learnt to walk upright. As babies, we still retain that primal desire to explore the world with our mouths, but as we grow we rapidly discover the full usefulness of our hands. In agility, flexibility and delicacy, they are far superior to dog paws. If your dog wants to grab your attention, she might clunk her front paw onto your knee. This is unlikely to be the most gentle of caresses. But if she wants to show you affection, she will lick you rather than attempt to stroke you.

We are told that dog's mouths are cleaner than ours. This makes some sense: they have a far wider aperture, and more circulating fresh air allows fewer opportunities for bugs to multiply. Also a dog's saliva contains certain antiseptics. However, this image of hygiene becomes somewhat diminished when we watch our dogs vigorously washing themselves or worse, hoovering up some other animals' faeces. Just for balance, human hands are rarely all that clean either.

God has blessed us, both humans and canines, with incredible bodies. Sometimes we need to contemplate another species, to appreciate the wonder of our construction. We might grumble when our backs hurt (apparently, we are still adapting to walking on two not four paws and our spines have yet to catch up fully). We might also despair at dogs' mouths when we find a treasured possession dented by canine tooth marks, but overall we should marvel and rejoice in the efficiency of design in our respective bodies.

And if we take delight in watching an older dog gently washing a pup, how much more delight might God take in us, when we use our hands for healing and our mouths for kindness? The psalmist wrote words which could be echoed by humans, dogs and all created beings alike:

'I praise you, for I am fearfully and wonderfully made.
Wonderful are your works, that I know very well.'

Psalm 139:14

 SOMETHING TO CHEW AS YOUR DOG WALKS ALONGSIDE YOU
How easy is it to contemplate God taking delight in us?

PART 2

EXPLORING 'THE ZONE'

4

'THE ZONE' PART 1 – GETTING LOST

'He's like a completely different dog when we're out and about with him.'

How does this happen? Your well-behaved, attentive dog becomes anything but, when taken out of the house and garden? Your nonsense words which prompt euphoria indoors, are met with blank indifference beyond the gate.

Sometimes the internet really does help. We found this pearl: 'When you're out, your dog could well be thinking *they* are taking *you* for a walk.' A lightbulb appeared, illuminating the root of this problem. Dogs have been bred from wolves, who operate in packs. When out on an adventure, one wolf leads the rest. And when you are top wolf (or dog), why listen to the bleatings of minors? At home, our dogs accept our authority, but out in the fields it might be a different matter. Whenever our dog enters this state of mind, when suddenly a new set of rules takes over, we say, 'He's gone into "the Zone".'

I have referred to 'the Zone' already and now it is time to examine it more closely. Technically there are many zones, but 'the

21

Zone' is a useful catch-all for when a dog sees a deer, catches a scent, hears a scurrying in the undergrowth, spots a rival or generally becomes over-stimulated to a point beyond normal recall. If your dog has not been neutered, you can add another all-consuming distraction to this list. The deeper they go into 'the Zone' the less we matter. They can still hear our voices (canine hearing is usually excellent) but like a drug addict in a crowded pub, haggling with their dealer, they focus on their quarry to the exclusion of everything else. It is a bit galling to be reduced to a non-essential, background noise, but this is what happens to all owners, when our dogs go deep into 'the Zone'.

As humans we are hardly immune from the power of 'the Zone'. We all have our preferred rabbit holes, into which we disappear. Some of these are clearly bad, such as Tik-Tok videos at mealtimes and far worse, 'the red mist', that murderous rage, whose descent renders us heedless of our usual constraints. Others are not so bad. We *should* have passions. It would be a tragedy to wander listlessly through life, steering clear of any deep engagements for fear of missing out on something else. The key thing is to avoid getting in so deep that we cannot surface again.

The reassuring news is that we can never be lost to God. Wherever we have gone and no matter how lost we have become, God never loses sight of us. When deep within 'the Zone' we lack any such awareness, for the Zone reduces God's voice to a background noise. Fortunately, God has an amazing track record for seeking and saving those unable to find their way home (more on this in the next few readings).

 Something to chew as your dog walks alongside you
Can I identify the occasions when my mind goes to a place, in which I completely forget that God is God?

SNIFF!
SNIFF!
SNIFF!

5
'THE ZONE' PART 2 –
BEING FOUND

It started in a Dagenham park. My Staffie-Labrador-cross had been with me for just over three weeks. As per the rescue shelter's advice, I had started letting him run around off the lead. All was going well until two mountainous black Newfoundlands lumbered over to say hello to him. His tail shot between his legs and after submitting to their sniffings, he slunk away, trotting at first and then bolting. I called but he did not look back. His fear had sent him deep into 'the Zone', far beyond my powers of recall. I watched him, tail still firmly lodged between his legs, dart out of the park gates and then, to my abject horror, onto a busy outer-London road. Quite how I don't know, but he found a gap through the traffic. I was not so fortunate. By the time I had reached the kerbside there was no break. And once I had finally crossed, he was nowhere to be seen.

Battling waves of panic, I tried to think logically. Where would he run? The most sensible answer was home. But when I arrived there ten minutes later, red faced and gasping for breath, he was not there. I lived in the middle of a terrace and so the front garden was the only place he could have been. What to do? I jumped onto my bike and spent a fruitless hour cycling around the streets. Whatever work I was supposed to be doing had gone straight out of the window. How could I contemplate settling to anything while my dog was missing? I cycled on and on, viewing every passing car as the one which might knock him down.

At last I returned home empty-handed, to pursue a new plan. I would start making calls and gather a search party. The phone was in my hand when I was interrupted by a knock at the door. It was my neighbour, Doris.

'Oh, Henry, there you are. I've been trying to get you for the last hour ...'

'I'm sorry, Doris. Can't it wait? I'm really busy.'

'It's just he won't budge.'

'Who won't?'

'*Your dog*. He's in our back garden and he won't move ...'

And there he was. He *had* returned home. But rather than waiting sensibly, he had been panicking and when our neighbours had opened their front door, he had barged past them, straight through their house and out the back.

He was happy to see me, but not noticeably more so than usual. He was back at home and so was I. All was well in his little world. His 'Zone' induced adventure was now behind him. My nerves took longer to resettle. I doubt if I did any work that day. Not that I cared. We were safely reunited. And I was so grateful, fully aware that not every lost-dog story ends this well.

Jesus tells several stories about searching until the lost are found; there is no real rest while coins, sheep and sons remain AWOL or when wounded strangers are lying unconscious in the gutter.[4] And if we're upset when our dogs are missing, how much more does God want us back, when we have disappeared so deeply into 'the Zone' that we cannot find our way home. The good news is, however lost we are, God sees us as too valuable to call off the search. Jesus, whose mission was seeking and saving the lost,[5] told stories that assure us that we can never become

[4] See Luke 15 (the whole chapter) and Luke 10:25-37.
[5] See Luke 19:10.

so lost that God cannot find us and restore us, to where we truly belong.

Something to chew as your dog walks alongside you
When singing 'Amazing Grace' what does the line, 'I once was lost but now I'm found' mean to me?
What are the specific details of my story?

'ISIS'

6

'THE ZONE' PART 3 – HOME, THE ANTIDOTE TO THE ZONE

Remember how, in the previous story, my runaway dog's anxieties vanished the moment we were reunited back at home? I would like to propose that 'Home' with a capital 'H' is the antidote to 'the Zone'.

When our dogs are at home (or in dog terms, in their den), they rarely lose themselves so deeply in 'the Zone'. Yes, they may get over-excited when a familiar visitor arrives, but it does not take them long to calm down again. The den is a safe place to relax, where scents are familiar and sounds are predictable. Perhaps there's less confusion about who is in charge, and so they experience less anxiety.

I enjoy the human-canine contrasts within *Downton Abbey*. Whenever the servants encounter the Earl of Grantham they bow or curtsey, often apologising for the intrusion of their presence. They skitter around the Abbey perpetually on eggshells, hyper-alert to any possible mistakes, such as a less than perfect uniform or an unmade fire. Isis, the Golden Labrador has a completely different experience. He ambles along at his own speed. If he finds the Earl, he wags his tail, wanders over and says hello before lying down and falling asleep. His calmness is the antithesis to the anxiety of the servants. The TV show is far too genteel to show genuine canine crudeness, but I very much doubt that Isis would suffer many qualms about farting or noisily washing himself, in front of his master. Dogs are like that and no wise human could ever take offence at such behaviour.

Dogs show us how created beings can be 'at home' in their own bodies. As humans, we waste ever increasing amounts of energy, in hating our shapes and feeling awkward about our physicality. Social media only accelerates this. Dogs don't do body-shaming in any form – not to us, not to other dogs and certainly not to themselves. I once read a book which advised me to brush my teeth before my prayer times, so that God would not have to endure my bad breath. I will concede that a minty mouth might help *my* mental preparations but I am quite certain that the Creator of sulphur, colons, sphincters, durian fruit and dung beetles is not going to be revolted by some mild halitosis.

God invites us to remove our usual masks and trust that our truest self is welcome and accepted. Being truly aware of God's presence is synonymous with being fully 'at Home'. It is deliverance from 'the Zone'. When we are alone with God, we are invited to make ourselves as 'at Home' as Isis is, in the Earl of Grantham's study. In that place, we understand that there is nothing we can do or say that will ever shock God. We can relax with our Alpha, lay down our preoccupations and adore. We can get excited about a friendly word, return the gaze of love and trust deeply that we are supremely welcome - just as we are. Downton's servants can never be truly 'at home' in the Abbey – Isis can. Jesus once said to his disciples:

> 'I do not call you servants any longer, because the servant does not know what the master is doing; but I have called you friends, because I have made known to you everything that I have heard from my Father.'[6]

[6] John 15:15.

Am I pushing my luck too far, to imagine him using this Isis of Downton analogy and saying, 'I see you more like dogs than servants, because in God's house you are welcomed and loved just by dint of being you?'

Something to chew as your dog walks alongside you
Could I cope with being as 'at Home' with God, as Isis is with the Earl of Grantham?

"THE RETURN OF THE POOCH"
(AFTER REMBRANDT)

7

'THE ZONE' PART 4 – BEING AT HOME WHEREVER WE ARE

What do we do when our dogs have disappeared deep in 'the Zone'? How can we help them? And if being 'at home' is the antidote to 'the Zone' how do we cope when we are far from the house?

When a darting hare sends our mutt deep into 'the Zone', we try all sorts of things. He remains by our side but in every other sense, he is very far from us. It is tempting to yell, especially if he catches us off guard and sends us staggering into a hedge. This does little to calm the situation. The same goes for jerking his lead to snap him out of it. The best medicine is to gently draw him back to us.

Step One is to calm him. Sometimes a stand-off is necessary before he sits down, but this is one of those times when persisting is important. All the while we speak to him, repeating his name and shamelessly plying him with treats to bring his attention back onto us. We know we have succeeded when he returns our eye contact and takes a treat gently. Then we fuss him, reminding him what a good boy he is before resuming our walk.

Jesus explained the power of a loving voice to his disciples. Sheep obey their shepherd's voice and the disciples obey his; he calls them by name and they return to him. Leonard Cohen illuminates this further. In one of his songs, he tries to entice the object of his infatuation into his arms. He calls to her, he calls to her but she does not answer. And then he realises his mistake; when he called, he had not done so softly enough.[7] Perhaps she had heard only his loudness and not his words? Perhaps she could not hear love at such a volume? Perhaps love can only be spoken gently? Can you imagine Jesus barking out a roll call of his sheep's names? And can we learn that our dogs respond better to a calm voice than a yell, especially when stuck deep in 'the Zone'? Coaxing them out, re-establishes the right relationship, where it is we who are in charge and not their desire for the hare. In other words, even out in the fields, calling them back to us, is calling them Home.

For Christians 'Home' is also less a place and more a state of being. We are most 'at Home', not necessarily when in our houses, but whenever we are alert to the presence of God. Richard Rohr once tweeted,

'We cannot attain the presence of God because we are already totally in the presence of God. What is absent is awareness.'[8]

By this reasoning, we can return 'Home' from wherever we find ourselves, without physically moving. All we need to do is quieten ourselves to the point where our ears can almost hear Jesus calling us by name, and as we respond, our right relationship resumes and the Zone's grip on us slackens.

 Something to chew as your dog walks alongside you
How can I grow in my awareness of God's presence? Who or what could teach me?

---

[7] 'Ain't no cure for love' by Leonard Cohen, 1988.
[8] @RichardRohrOFM, on Twitter 10 January 2013.

PART 3

HUMANS AND DOGS
LIVING TOGETHER

8

THE WOLF PACT

Around 15,000 years ago[9] a pact began. A few wolves decided that hanging out around humans gave them a better chance of survival than sticking exclusively with their fellows. They surrendered the familiar safeties of the wild pack, for the promises of better protection and more food from their new, non-lupine leaders. Humans benefited from new hunting assistants who doubled as security guards for their encampments.

As this pact evolved, humans took control of their breeding, favouring the friendlier over the distrusting and the gentler over the aggressive. Eventually, litter by litter, they became a separate species, genetically well disposed towards humans. The deal forged way back then, is still on; in the simplest terms, both protect each other; dogs give humans service and humans give dogs food and shelter.

I can spend far too much time watching videos online. The algorithms that power my social media networks have figured out that I enjoy short films in which an appallingly malnourished mutt is rescued from some gutter and slowly rehabilitated into a well-groomed playful pet. The thing that never fails to amaze me, is how

[9]   Or 12,000 years ago, or 33,000 years ago; there are a wide range of opinions on this.

even the most abused dogs still hold an innate trust of humans. Despite the worst provocations, they can never relinquish those friendly genes inherited from the former wolves with whom the pact was first made.

Whether that pact can be called a covenant is a matter for debate. Certainly nothing was ever written down and there was no signing ceremony, but nevertheless the two species entered into a mutually beneficial arrangement that exists to this day. Only we humans are not doing so well at keeping our side. Too many dogs are mistreated, abandoned or allowed to keep on breeding beyond human capacity to care for their pups.

We are on cheerier ground when we think about the various covenants God has made with humans: spoken, graven, inscribed, enshrined and even written directly onto our human hearts.[10] How *mutually* beneficial these are, is a mystery and we'll ponder what God might get out of these another day. Humans do extremely well out of these deals. We are given a status as children of God, made with love and for love. We are invited to a place at God's table. We are able to speak with God directly, without intermediaries; and this privilege is not confined to temples, shrines or hill tops, neither is it the exclusive preserve of the powerful, be they moneyed, royal or ordained. Each of us can call out to God and expect to be heard, no matter who we are, what we have done or what kind of mess we are in.

The testimony of Bible writers and beyond, is that God's side of the deal is well kept. The same Bible writers are unanimous in owning our continual human failures to keep our side well. If dogs could talk, some might chip in that our covenant-keeping with them is often found wanting. God is incredibly forgiving of our breaches – and so are our dogs. Such grace should not be taken lightly.

 Something to chew as your dog walks alongside you
What deals does God make with us? And what does God want from us?

10 Jeremiah 31:31-33.

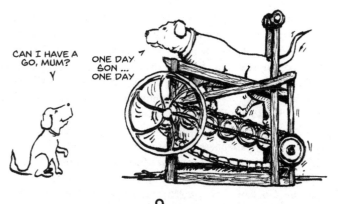

9

BEING USEFUL

For most of canine-human history dogs have had clearly defined uses. Their jobs justified their upkeep. Humans engineered different breeds for specific purposes. Many revolved around hunting: spaniels, setters, pointers, retrievers, bloodhounds and so on all enhanced the human ability to kill other animals. Even the docile, long-eared basset hound was originally a hunter; humans wanted something with short legs that would assist while not running too far ahead. Greyhounds were bred on that same principle, albeit reversed; their long legs made them faster than deer. Humans took dogs with territorial traits to create mastiffs, beaucerons and German shepherds to guard their property. We mated intelligent dogs with compliant dogs to produce collies; perhaps humanity's ultimate canine co-worker. We developed bulldogs and bull terriers for sport; although 'sport' cannot possibly be the correct word for the vile 'entertainment' of baiting badgers or attacking a chained-up bull. In nineteenth-century France, dogs were trained to run in treadmills, which in turn operated bellows for the forges of domestic nail makers. Older dogs taught the trade to the next generation of pups.[11] Such dogs were highly valued and their humans never questioned why they fed and looked after them.

[11] *The Discovery of France*, Graham Robb, Picador, 2007, p. 167.

Most of these jobs have been lost, mainly due to advances in technology. There is also a growing revulsion with cruelty. Guarding and sheep herding remain, sledging, hunting and retrieving less so and carting now belongs firmly in the past. Highly trained dogs make invaluable companions for disabled people and careers in sniffing are booming as humans explore new possibilities for the canine sense of smell. For some, dogs function as substitute children. Julian Clary subverts this by claiming that his canine companions are substitute *parents*, bringing calmness and clarity to his life.[12]

You might think that the loss of useful employment would see a decrease in the global canine population. The truth is quite the opposite. Dogs are now valued for something more than economics. Humans want dogs just for their dog-selves. This is not entirely new. Centuries ago Chinese nobles bred pugs purely as pets. Queen Victoria developed pomeranians for no other purpose than the enjoyment of having them around. Most dogs today have only one job: full time companions to humans.

We might wonder what use we are as humans. The planet does not need us. In fact, it tends to thrive in those few remaining places that we have yet to touch. God surely does not need us, in the sense that God could carry on being God perfectly well without us. So why did God make us? Perhaps we have been created less for specific usefulness, and more so that God can enjoy our company. We do have tasks, duties and obligations; we are to care for each other (and for the planet) with justice, mercy, peace and humility. But even though our actions often fall short, our prime calling remains: to exist as God's companions, even more loved than our dogs are loved by us.

Something to chew as your dog walks alongside you

How often do I value myself in terms of my work, my work-related status and my perceived use? And in contrast, how does God value me?

---

[12] *The Lick of Love: How Dogs Changed My Life*, Julian Clary, Quercus Publishing, 2021.

10

OVER-BREEDING AND UNDER-BREATHING

I once had the following conversation with a nine-year-old:

Me: When you're older, do you think you'll own a dog?
9yo: Oh yes! I want a pug.
Me: A pug? Goodness! And why do you want a pug?
9yo: Because they look so cute. Their faces are so sweet.
Me: Do you know sometimes pugs have trouble breathing, because they are born with noses so squashed they can't get enough air through them?
9yo: (*after a pause*) But they look so cute! I want one.

Certain features tug on our human heartstrings. With pugs it is a large head with a flat round face and big eyes. This is called the 'baby schema effect' and cartoonists have been pressing this button in us for years, from Bambi to Pokémon and beyond. And we should be grateful: this trait encouraged our parents and other adults to care for us when we were very small. Dogs have less reason to be glad. Sometimes their cute looks are valued more highly than their everyday health. We have now so overdeveloped certain breeds that they struggle to breathe. Too many French and English bulldogs, along with pugs are born, condemned to a lifelong battle for air. Their deformed skulls can also be damaging to their eyes. Dogs like having dog noses, not stubby human-sized snouts. When they cannot draw in enough oxygen, they exercise less and consequently pile on weight. The situation is getting worse as over breeding continues, and breathlessness is considered normal. It is not just flat-faced breeds which suffer; a dachshund's long, low body may look cute, but it puts them at risk of both spinal and neurological problems. [13] Well-meaning but naïve, dog-loving humans spend huge sums on new pups and thus sustain the industry. The cruel irony is ghastly; the teeny trotting legs and sweet round faces that trigger our caring responses are also prompting us to perpetuate suffering.

Genesis tells us that God has appointed humans as stewards over Creation. This is a task at which we fail disastrously, continually placing our short-term gains ahead of our holy duties. Our overbreeding of certain dogs is but one symptom of our neglect and might be harder to spot, because it comes ready-wrapped in a warm blanket of sentimentality. But in the stark light of day, there is nothing kind about planning another litter of asphyxiating pups, no matter how cute they might look. God is love and we can only do God's work with kindness, but kindness alone is never enough. We also need to be wise. Kindness without wisdom can be a very dangerous thing. Alexandra Horowitz has issued a rallying cry: we should value breeds not for purity but for health, swapping 'purebred' for 'healthbred' as the buzzword.[14]

The answer is simple, too simple for many to countenance: we need to realign our compassion so that it works more for dogs and less for our sentimental delight. Dogs already have the solution. Just watch them in a park. They could not care less about selective breeding, often to the dismay of their owners. And when a snub-

[13] The BVA (British Veterinary Association) offers the following advice: 'Avoid buying a pet bred with extreme designer features and choose a healthier breed or non-pedigree animal instead', www.bva.co.uk.
[14] *Our Dogs, Ourselves,* Alexandra Horowitz, Simon & Schuster, 2019, p. 135.

nosed thoroughbred gets cosy with some shaggy pedigree-free mutt, their mongrel pups will have longer snouts. And be healthier for it. And no less beautiful.

Something to chew as your dog walks alongside you
When else might kindness without wisdom, lead us away from obedience to God?

'ERIC'

11
ALPHAS AND EQUALS

Do you ever wonder what your dog is thinking? Would you be shocked to discover that it might have half an eye on your overthrow? Our captive, domesticated companions still hear the whispers of their wolf ancestors: the expectation that one day, they will breed and, with their mate, share the charge of their own pack. In the true wild, wolves generally live in family units run by Mum and Dad. When their pups mature, they leave to form new packs. In captivity, confined together with unrelated wolves, they develop a more distinct notion of hierarchy, characterised by domineering alphas and non-breeding subordinates. There are many myths surrounding these structures, leading to some wild theories about human alpha males, but these all derive from restricted wolves and not from their free cousins.

So what of our beloved pooches? They are lifelong captives in human-made packs and very far from the wild. As such, when they feel those ancient lupine urges, they might embark on some domineering behaviour and challenge their alphas. Even if they do not, their minds have not been constructed to accommodate human notions of equality. If we offer them these, they will misinterpret our meaning. I often wish it was otherwise, but I concede to the saying, 'Treat your dog as a human and it'll treat you as a dog.'

If we allow them up onto the sofa 'just the once', they will soon consider this privilege as their right, *and* a valuable step up the ladder. It is for humans to choose where the lines are drawn. Some allow the sofa, some even the bed. Whatever we decide, we should not allow our captive wolf descendant any delusions about who is in charge. A friend admitted that her dog never responded well to her authority. Then she reflected on her behaviour, in particular the amount of playtime she spent, rolling around on the floor, letting the dog stand over her. To her, this was a fun game. To her dog, it was a signal of her lower rank within the captive pack. I saw a TV documentary about a dog who had become incredibly aggressive, especially at mealtimes. It transpired that his owner used to stage mock standoffs with him. The human would put the food bowl on the floor and then crouch over it, pretending to growl. The dog growled back and so the two of them carried on, until the human got bored and let the dog eat. To the human, this was a fun game. To the dog, this was a rival backing down. The human was teaching a disastrous lesson; in this pack you fight for your food and whoever wins is the alpha.

Food is important. One of our best ways of reinforcing our status as leaders, is to create rituals over feeding, such as requiring a dog sit near to their full bowl and wait for our spoken permission before eating. Such exercises can feel petty. We might ask ourselves, 'Am I really so inadequate that I need bolster my flagging self-esteem by lording it over my dog in this way?' That, however, is to misunderstand the hierarchical mind-set of your captive wolf descendent. It is *never* our job to be unkind, and it is an unkindness to allow a dog to imagine that the alpha slot is attainable. When treated with fair, consistent rules, dogs will settle happily into their correct, lower place within our household packs.

Given all this, we humans might expect our infinitely superior God to be equally firm with us, barking orders to keep us in line. Instead, we find ourselves treated us with exceptional grace. This might at times be confusing to us, due to the way our minds are constructed: we are also pack animals, ever watchful of our shifting statuses within our human hierarchies and often with more than half an eye on our own advancement. Instead of being pushed down, we find ourselves invited to sit at God's table and encouraged to speak without fear. But we can allow ourselves no delusions that we have earned this seat, or worse still, have somehow won it by conquest. Our elevation comes to us by grace alone. Christians believe that in Christ, God came to us in great humility, but we cross a serious line if we ever view the Servant King as our personal run-around. The Bible contains some dizzying passages (surely grist to an egotistical mill) promising us golden crowns and the power to judge angels.[15] I cannot begin to envisage what this latter might look like in practice. And I shy away from too much speculation, lest I become so dazzled that I forget that all my good things are ultimately gifts from God. In our relationship with God, we are privileged beyond our wildest imaginings, but we will never reach the status of equals, and any fantasies in which we act as 'The Alpha' are simply dangerous.

Something to chew as your dog walks alongside you
Are we allowed up onto God's sofa? And if so, on what terms?

---

[15] 1 Corinthians 6:3.

GREYFRIARS
BOBBY!
ABSOLUTE
LEGEND

12

UNDERDOGS

Question: What makes us, as humans, better than the animals – dogs included?

Answer: The question is flawed. It assumes a false division. Humans *are* animals.

Humans often forget this. We often regard all other animals as our underdogs, even though we, like them, all evolved from the same ocean-dwelling microorganisms. Dogs, geese, moths, conifers, daffodils, toadstools and tardigrades all started in the same place. We might claim to have developed further than any other species, but even if this were true, does it entitle us to treat the so called 'humbler creation' as we please, with impunity?

We have bigger brains than our dogs, but this alone should not make them underdogs. Sperm whales have huge brains and we never consider deferring to them. In the past, we relied on religious books to justify our superiority. Texts written by human scribes asserted that humans had immortal souls and 'animals' did not. Later, philosophers posited that our gift of language set us apart and above. But humans stating that humans are the best is not a sound process.

If dolphins set the normative standard, they would squeak at our claims. 'Superior race? What kind of superior race comes with no built-in bio sonar?' Ravens might quork, 'They can't even fly.' And then the butterflies might flap forward with, 'And zero ability to see ultraviolet light. What a shambles!' And if ultraviolet vision, flying and bio sonar were the most important criteria, then the crown for top species would go to ... bats. Dogs would intervene however, upholding the value of a highly-developed sense of smell.

The truth is that humans *are* the best ... but only when it comes to being human. By many other measures, we fall behind. Collectively, we are the most powerful species on this planet, but if that is the main basis for our claim, then we risk saying 'might is right' ... and that leads to a catalogue of calamities.

How else might we define superiority? Rabbi Jonathan Wittenberg explores the 'wavelength of the heart'. Within this, humans are often the underdogs: actual dogs excel far beyond us in love and joie de vivre. He removes the sting from the discussion, by replacing competition with collaboration: we are better *with* dogs. When they are alongside us, our eyes are opened to a wider, more connected world.[16]

In the superiority game, there is only one clear winner, and that is God, who surpasses all created life, in ability, intellect, creativity, power and love. And as for our human brains, God does not consider these our most useful asset. According to Jesus' parable of the sheep and the goats, the deciding questions at the final judgement will be about not be about our loaf, but rather our love: how we treated the hungry, the thirsty, the stranger, the naked, the sick and the prisoner.[17] It seems God values the 'wavelength of the heart' over intellectual dexterity and doctrinal correctness, which are barely also-rans, not meriting a mention in Jesus' story. As to our superior collective power, Jesus elsewhere warns that power must be only exercised within the bounds of love, i.e. wisely, kindly and with humility. Rulers and tyrants may lord it over their subjects and kick them around as underdogs, but Jesus forbids his followers

---

[16]   *Things My Dog Has Taught Me About Being a Better Human*, Jonathan Wittenberg, Hodder & Stoughton, 2017, p. 65.
[17]   Matthew 25:31-46.

from ever behaving like that.[18] At this point he is speaking about how humans treat humans, but I suspect that we will be held to similar expectations, when being judged for our treatment of God's less collectively powerful animals. In God's Kingdom, underdogs find unexpected honours.

This has got heavy today. Let's end with a dog story. Bobby, a Skye Terrier was the devoted pet of John Gray. When John died, Bobby continued to love him. Legend maintains that Bobby remained loyally by his master's grave in Edinburgh's Greyfriar's Kirkyard, for a further fourteen years. The locals came to respect Bobby's devotion, keeping him fed and paying for his license, until he himself died and was buried nearby. Then they erected a statue in his honour. Certain details of this story are sometimes questioned, but the loyalty of dogs is not. Nor is their capacity for love.

 Something to chew as your dog walks alongside you
How might I expand the wavelength of my heart?

13

SUBMISSION

Dogs might have no words but they still have many ways of showing us respect. In the wild, defeated wolves will lie down on their backs before their victor, displaying their bellies. This is their way of saying, 'OK, you're ahead of me. I present no threat to your status.' Our dogs do similar things, mercifully more often in play than in actual combat. Two dogs at their first meeting might enjoy a wild time, establishing which is dominant in a reasonably cordial manner. We should not dismiss such games as frivolous just because they are having fun.

They show their submission to us in a variety of ways: licking our hands or our mouths (if we let them), flattening their ears, tucking away their tails, averting their gaze to avoid eye contact, submissive peeing and stretching out their front legs to perform a 'play bow'. These are all traits handed down from their wolf ancestors. We should welcome these (OK, maybe not the peeing) because they show us that our pet is not planning any shake up of the existing hierarchy.

As humans, we also possess a variety of ways of demonstrating our submission to God. We bow our heads to pray. We might kneel to confess or receive communion. Some even go so far as to prostrate themselves on the ground. This is small stuff when compared to our biblical predecessors who tore their clothes, thumped their chests and covered their heads with ashes. Jesus in the Lord's Prayer encourages our submission with a daily reminder that God's ways and God's will are preferable to ours, 'Your Kingdom come, your will be done'. St Paul advocates offering our bodies as living sacrifices so that our minds may be transformed.[19] Our hymns constantly affirm and reaffirm our secondary status to God:

> 'I am weak but Thou art strong'
> 'Take my life and let it be, consecrated, Lord, to Thee'
> 'We fall down'
> 'I surrender all'

and we sing about a time when we will cast down our golden crowns into a glassy sea before the throne of God.

In all of this, we do well to remember that submission to God is not the same as submission to the Church and its hierarchies. Our dogs accord us a level of trust, which we would be unwise to emulate in our dealings with any human authorities, be they politicians, police officers or religious ministers. As humans, they are fallible and poorly equipped to shoulder such a burden. And any pastor who permits discrimination, who equates taking a vaccine with a lack of faith, who fails to respond appropriately to a report of abuse or who expects us to empty our savings into their vaults, is not worthy of our trust. Dogs seem unable to make such distinctions, instead they continue to obey even as they are being mistreated. At such times they need others (i.e. us) to intervene and protect them.

Also it is worth noting that in dogs, submission and fear share the same outward signs. Submissive *and* intimidated dogs keep their tails tucked away. We want our dogs' greeting dance to be a dance of joy, not of anxiety. And how much more does God desire us to approach with wagging tails, alert ears and a bounce that says that we are both submissive *and* fully confident of our welcome.

[19] Romans 12:1-2.

Something to chew as your dog walks alongside you
Have I ever offered my complete submission to something less than God? And have I ever unfairly required someone's else submission to my will?

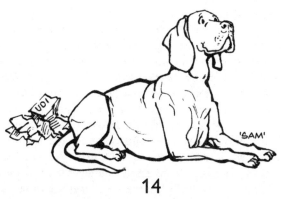

14

DEPENDENCE

Have you ever suffered the guilty realisation that no one fed the dog last night? 'But I thought you did it!' we say out loud to our partners, before adding under our breaths, 'It was kind of your turn'. Meanwhile the poor dog just wants food. I don't have children, but I'm fairly sure I would never forget to feed them. They would tell me. Or if they were teenagers, they would just help themselves from the fridge. Our dogs can do neither. If we do not feed them, no one else will. They are completely dependent on us.

As adults, we would not enjoy this set up. We value our concept of independence. We like to tell ourselves, 'We are the captains of our own ships.' Some people hop up and down on their keyboards, blasting across social media, 'I've worked hard for everything I've got and I've never benefitted from one single handout.' In their minds this is clearly a virtue (and all too often a lead-up to an angry put-down of others, usually immigrants). Scroll down through the replies to where some brave soul reminds them that their education, health care and protection from crime have all been provided for them[20] … and then enjoy their self-righteous rebuttals. Truth on such occasions is rarely welcome. Dogs do not share this need to 'make

[20] This is true at least for citizens of Western European countries.

it on my own'. And before God, their stance is the better one.

A lawyer approaches Jesus with the question, 'What must I do to inherit eternal life?' Jesus does not give a straight answer, but tells a magnificent parable about a badly wounded man, ignored by the religious establishment and rescued by a distrusted foreigner. The lawyer needs to rethink his question. Whatever versions of eternity lie within his earning capacity, can only be cheap shams compared with God's version. Our entry into the next life, depends entirely on God, just as the wounded man's rescue depends on the Samaritan.[21] In a different parable, Jesus confronts our treasured fantasies of independence within this life. He tells of a rich man, who hoards good things to guarantee a comfortable future but foolishly forgets that he will die one day. And when that day comes, his wealth is no help to him.[22] Like it or not, we are utterly dependent on God for everything. 'Daily bread' means much more than food.

We might baulk at this, but perhaps this is where we can learn from our dogs. They cheerfully accept their dependence on us, and how much more should we discard our wan unilateral delusions of independence from God and instead, receive with generous hearts all that God so freely gives?

 Something to chew as your dog walks alongside you
Do I ever resent my level of dependence on God?

---

21   The Parable of the Good Samaritan, Luke 10:25-37.
22   The Parable of the Rich Fool, Luke 12:13-21.

'JARVIS'

15

RELIANCE

Some of us become very dependent on our dogs, and not just for daily companionship. Certain highly-trained dogs are to us, a living key, opening doors to a wider world.

Jarvis was a natural seeing dog. He accompanied Dave on countless expeditions, making the outside world so much more accessible for him. From their very first walk, Dave knew that Jarvis was special. Jarvis's trainer was with them, wanting to see how Jarvis performed. He did very well. He guided Dave expertly through the town centre, following each of Dave's instructions and responding well to Dave's voice. He did not allow himself to be distracted at all. Then came the moment when Dave wanted to cross a road. Jarvis took him to a pedestrian crossing, where they waited. Now one of Dave's things is that, when standing still at a kerbside, he sometimes rocks backwards and forwards, unsure of his balance. Jarvis noticed this and without any command, placed his whole body directly in front of Dave's knees, giving him some reassuring stability. Dave had not come across anything like this before, and he asked the trainer if this was a new feature in guide dogs' training. 'No, not at all,' came the reply. It seems that Jarvis had seen a need *and* understood how he could meet it. Dave knew from this moment that he could rely on Jarvis and the two of them enjoyed a long and happy relationship, as owner and guide.

If we rely on our dogs, does God rely on us? We have certain tasks which have been entrusted to us. We are to act as stewards within God's creation. We are to love one another, especially keeping in mind those at the margins. God cares for all of us, but it falls to us to deliver a great deal of that caring ourselves. We are not supposed to sit praying for miraculous interventions for problems we can solve ourselves. God gave Jarvis the intelligence to take the initiative. God has given us humans even more: we have ways of sharing knowledge and companions so that we can work collectively and we have a hotline to God, for when we need guidance. The following poem, usually attributed to St Teresa of Ávila, seeks to capture our delegated responsibilities:

> 'Christ has no body now but yours. No hands, no feet on earth but yours. Yours are the eyes through which he looks with compassion on this world. Yours are the feet with which he walks to do good. Yours are the hands through which he blesses all the world. Yours are the hands, yours are the feet, yours are the eyes, you are his body. Christ has no body now on earth but yours.'

To me it makes far better sense if we understand the much repeated 'yours' as a plural not a singular, otherwise it becomes unduly burdensome: I have grown suspicious of how wannabe lone superheroes fit into God's plans. Two, but preferably more, working together are usually far more fruitful than one going it alone. And our dogs show us that we can rely on others from beyond our own species.

 Something to chew as your dog walks alongside you
Can it really be that God relies on us?

16
TOYS

RIP Turtle (squeaker included)

Ripped into pieces while still in your prime, your packaging promised that you would last for three years, but you barely managed three weeks. First your tail and then your legs went, one by one. The final indignity was the breaching of your body, leading to the evisceration of your internal fluff and the liberation of your plastic squeaker. Fearing you might wreak a posthumous revenge by choking our dog, we retired you fully (and wondered whether we had kept your receipt).

There is something both endearing and tragic about a dog's pride in its toys. The sense of 'tragic' grows as the pride remains but the toys diminish, both in cleanliness and in limbs. Even near their endings, they are collected, treasured and paraded around. They are thrust at visitors, who if properly trained will express due amazement. The dog, happily wagging says (at least according to my anthropomorphising imagination), 'Yes. I *do* have one of these. And it's mine. Do you want it? Ha! You can't have it! You can chase me if you'd like, but it *will* remain mine.' When this scenario involves other dogs, fights might ensue. A visiting dog might only learn the hard way which toys are to be shared and which are only to be gazed at in awestruck jealousy.

We look with a mixture of fond curiosity and mild incomprehension at our dogs' obvious delight in their scruffy, faded and tooth-pocked bits of plastic. And I have to ask what does God make of us, as we ooh and aah over something as transient as a car, or an item of clothing (or dare I say, even a painting)? No doubt our ancestors enjoyed a surge of dopamine on returning to the cave clutching a new item, never imagining the problems this would cause us in this age of super-abundance. We attach huge importance to our possessions, frequently spending far more money on merely insuring them than we give to our fellow humans in need. Granny Weatherwax once upbraided a young monk with the lesson that sin is treating people like things.[23] And I'd add '… and things like people'. Does God expect us to live without owning things? We would find it hard. Our toys bring us much pleasure. The danger comes when we cling to them, unwilling to share and refusing to let go when their usefulness has passed. Turning to another work of fantasy, we find the Elven Queen, Galadriel blessing Gimli the dwarf, foretelling that his hands will flow with gold, whilst reassuring that gold will never have dominion over him.[24] Her blessing appeals to me, containing as it does, the implicit warning that possessions can possess us. They can also deaden us to God's reminder that we cannot take any of them with us.

There is a horrible irony that our western dogs often own more toys than many of the world's children. I once saw a group of lads in Uganda chasing around after a lumpen 'football' made from rubbish tied up with string. The answer is not to deprive our dogs, but to work together, praying and protesting for a better deal … a fair deal for all … and toys for all our children.

[23] *Carpe Jugulum*, Terry Pratchett, Doubleday, 1998.
[24] *The Fellowship of the Ring*, J. R. R. Tolkien, Allen & Unwin, 1954.

Something to chew as your dog walks alongside you
Is my attitude towards any of my precious 'toys' ever harmful to my spiritual health?

17

DOGTOPIA

Sometimes I wonder how well this relationship is working for our dogs? The Wolf Pact formed by our ancestors still pays huge dividends to us humans. But I have to ask if even our most pampered pooches, are truly living their best dog lives? Is the modern human household a good substitute for the lupine pack? As humans we continue our daily lives, in our human-centric world, designed and sustained to suit us. (How well it works for all humans is another matter.) Dogs however have been lifted out of the wolf world and placed into another that is often a poor fit. Sometimes I look at our dog and wonder how I would answer him, if he made the following observations:

- I have very limited contact with other *proper* dogs (as opposed to you weird ape-like, bipedal dogs).
- I am often unaccountably left alone, which feels like rejection from our pack.
- I cannot hunt and I only eat at times of your choosing.
- I walk restrained by your lead.
- I get told off for being a dog: welcoming guests, sniffing around, marking territory and searching for food (and if you don't want

me to go through the bins, how about NOT burying intriguing scents inside them?).

- I don't get to play as much as I'd like. You're often too busy staring at your illuminated screens.
- I retain a primal instinct to breed and lead my own family pack, however I am unable to pass on my DNA because you humans removed this ability from me without my consent.

It is quite a list. Mercifully our dogs do not bear such grudges. Even when hurt, they have an astonishing capacity for forgiveness, or at least moving on. They may be perpetual teenagers, but they seem to be mercifully free from the prolonged sulking we experience in human adolescence.

In an ideal world, our pack would be made up of a wonderful, motley collection of humans and hounds. The humans would see to all those exclusively human-to-human issues, and the dogs to theirs. And all other needs would be met by a happy combined effort, from humans and canines living in symbiotic harmony. This would be utopia … or maybe 'dogtopia'.

I have answers for all the issues in my non-verbal dog's imagined list and they are perfectly reasonable answers … but I am a human and can only guess at a dog's perspective. I retain the ace of trumps, 'Do you remember what it was like in the rescue centre? Good! Now consider how many more dogs dream of making it even to there. You have so much here.' Playing the others-have-it-so-much-worse card, might shut down a complainant, but it does not satisfy all their complaints. Perhaps it would be better to explain that nothing is perfect in this world and demanding that it should be is a sure-fire route to frustrated disappointment. It is good to aim high, but maybe not to insist on perfection.

We, equally could come to God with a very long list of gripes, bewailing the many inadequacies of this present dispensation. We can find endless faults in the world, society and Church, and if we are honest, within ourselves. Some things are fixable. We might be able to reverse the Climate Emergency, we can limit corruption in politics, we can radically reduce the sufferings of animals[25] and we can start retrieving the 171 trillion pieces of plastic we have dumped into our oceans. But we will not cure every disease, we will not abolish ageing nor will we dodge dying and the poor will always be with us. God remains invisible and at times might appear woefully inactive. This world is far from perfect. But if we can accept this, we will find there is much to enjoy.

Utopia remains beyond our grasp. Dogtopia likewise. We can and should strive for better, and while we do this, we could also pop on our boots and take the dog out for a walk. And perhaps remember as we go, that God walks with us too.

Something to chew as your dog walks alongside you
How can we balance the quest for better with gratitude for good-enough?

---

[25] Just one of too many examples of human awfulness to animals; 'Hog-towers' are 26-floor megafarms in Hubei province, able to raise and slaughter more than a million pigs a year, while in the US 99 per cent of animals raised for food live in factory farms. 'China's Pig High-Rises Are Horrifying. So Are America's Factory Farms', *The New Republic*, Jan Dutkiewicz, February 15, 2023.

PART 4

INSTRUCTIONS

HEEL!
HEEL!
HEEL!
HEEL!
(SHEEESH)

18

HOW MANY TIMES DO I NEED TO TELL YOU?

Out of all the instructions we give to our dog, 'heel' seems to be our favourite. If we logged our every imperative, and ranked them according to the number of times each is issued, 'heel' would top our chart. On a bad day, it is issued at every fifth step, with me fearing that constant repetition is rendering it utterly meaningless.

At the other end of the scale is the command 'go'. At feeding time, this needs saying only once. He expects it. He listens for it, giving unwavering eye contact. Sometimes he is so keen to obey, he tries to set off before the word is given.

In between 'heel' and 'go' are instructions such as 'come here', 'sit' and 'lie down'. These meet with varying levels of compliance, usually related to the proximity of treats.

I wonder, as we walk with God each day, which commands we meet with eager anticipation and which we are most adept at ignoring? A couple of years ago I compiled a list of all the imperatives issued by Jesus across all four gospels. I expected 'love' to be the most repeated, but it is not. If you accept 'take courage' and 'do not fear' as being in essence, the same command, their variants come in second place. 'Let' and 'take', again with variants ('take note', 'take nothing', 'take up') are also popular. I counted only three times when Jesus told someone to 'sit'. 'Leap' appears just the once. None of this was very scientific. I made no reference to the original Greek and no allowance for repetitions of the same stories across the different gospels. I was simply seeking a rough overview.

Jesus certainly got fed up with issuing the same instructions to his unreceptive disciples. At one point he said, 'Why do you call me, "Lord, Lord," and do not do what I say?'[26] He then proceeded to tell a story about wise and foolish builders, finishing with the warning of an impending crash, for those who ignore his words.

For the record, the instruction Jesus uses more than any other is, 'go'. Maybe we as disciples are less receptive to 'go' than our dogs and therefore need to be told more often. But 'love', despite being issued as an imperative only eight times, still wins overall as the most important, since it is the end goal of all the others; Jesus summarises, 'I am giving you these commands so that you may love one another.'[27]

I issue instructions to my dog for a variety of reasons: a mixture of my love for him *and* my desire for an easy walk. Jesus tells us to do things, less for his benefit and much more for ours, that we might love one another, build well together and avoid painful crashes.

Something to chew as your dog walks alongside you
Out of all of God's instructions, to which do I respond the best? And which does God need to repeat over and over?

26   Luke 6:46.
27   John 15:17.

19

HANGING ON
EVERY WORD

Jesus tells us that poor listening leads to poor results, especially when it comes to listening to him. Those who have ears need to use them well, to hear everything he is saying. In his parable of the sower, he describes four types of listening. Those who offer stony indifference, receive no benefit at all. Those who half-listen to him whilst letting the other half of their attention wander elsewhere, find his message ends up like young plants choked by weeds. His words equally fail to thrive amongst those who hear but only in a shallow way – in one ear and out of the other. As plants, they fail to take root and get frazzled by the midday sun. Out of his four options, only one succeeds; those who listen carefully, giving Jesus their full, undivided attention reap a harvest.[28] So what does this type of listening look like in practice? I used to say it was like a wedding couple hearing each other's vows, but now I have a better analogy.

If you have a dog in your house, go and pick up their treat bag, but try to do this as quietly as possible. You know what will happen

[28] The Parable of the sower, Matthew 13:1–23, Mark 4:1–20, Luke 8:4–15.

next. Your dog will appear instantly. Where treats are concerned they always give that fourth kind of listening. How would our lives look if we were so attuned to the sounds of Jesus?

Of course dogs fulfil the other three listening scenarios too. For shallow listening, try using a new command on a puppy after only a couple of training sessions. For the weeds, ask your dog to sit and focus solely on you when there's a butterfly nearby. As for the stony path … when I was a vicar, I once missed a school assembly because my then dog decided to extend his morning walk. He blanked my increasingly urgent calls to return, leaving me (in my dog collar) yelling, 'I know you can hear me', while he (in his dog collar) trotted off, sniffing at whatever took his fancy.

Contrast that frustration with the delight of having a dog respond well to your every word. It's true they are most likely to do this when there's food involved. But could this not be the same for us, if Jesus really is, as he claims, the bread of life? The more we believe in him, the more alert we are to the rustle of his movements and the more fruitful our lives become.

 Something to chew as your dog walks alongside you
What would a human life look like, if someone truly heard, received and obeyed every word spoken to them by Jesus?

20

REWARDS

Dogs do things for rewards. It really is that simple. Our dog is entirely food-focused. Having only had Labrador crosses I was amazed to discover that there are dogs who are *not* food-focused. How can this be? Fortunately for us this makes him very easy to reward. Other dogs require different approaches, namely even more praise and attention. Of course all dogs need these too, and since praise strengthens the relationship it is ultimately more important than treats.

Talk of rewards takes me back to the prison where I was a chaplain. One afternoon, I was part of a multi-disciplinary group, convened to talk with a man whose behaviour was spectacularly bad. He did not remain in the meeting for long. He rapidly became so abusive that he had to be returned to his cell. We sat looking at each other. I was clueless as to why anyone would act like this. And then the psychologist asked a question that lit a light bulb in my head: 'What kind of rewards does he seek?' This made immediate sense to me. I realised how close we are to dogs. We do things for rewards. It really is that simple. Most, if not all our actions are orientated around rewards. The daily grind? If we are lucky we turn up for job satisfaction, failing that, we exchange our effort for money ... we all have bills to pay. Rough patches in relationships? We endure these in the hope that things will get better. Volunteering in our free time? We find companionship with like-minded people. And so on.

But back in prison what possible rewards could this man glean from behaving so badly? And I do mean badly. The answer might be as simple as ... attention. We all need attention. Oscar Wilde once quipped, 'There is only one thing in life worse than being talked about, and that is not being talked about.' We are social animals. If no one ever pays us attention, we might find ourselves facing that ultimate horror ... meaninglessness. The man in prison had learnt that being difficult rewarded him with a great amount of attention from staff and a certain notoriety from his fellow prisoners. Tragically, he seemed to have abandoned any hope of gaining positive attention. Perhaps his childhood attempts had never been rewarded?

If we want our dogs to act in a certain way, we need to ask, 'Is what we're asking of them, rewarding for them?' The immediate answer is possibly, 'No'. The suitable-for-humans-behaviour we demand usually requires the suppression of some deeply rooted canine instinct, such as chasing a hare, rolling in ick or clinging to a newly found treasure. If we want them to defy their natures for our benefit, we have to reward their every obedient decision. Treats are good but most of all, we need to lavish them with praise, remembering that we only have a two-second window in which they will connect our response with their action. For this we need to be observant and never take their good choices for granted.

We have more capacity than dogs, both to plan ahead and to offset current slog against future recompense. But ultimately, we share with dogs the same prime motivation: we behave in ways that we hope will bring rewards. We might insist that virtue is its own reward, but that only reiterates the point – we like rewards.

What rewards come from living with God? Do these match the rewards we find through religious observance? Let's imagine a Venn diagram, showing how religious activities can fall both within and beyond God's desires. Religious observance can reward us with fellowship, guidance, healing, purpose, the assurance of forgiveness and love. It also dispenses status, busy-ness and a sense of security within familiar traditions. Some churches offer a kind of doctrinal certainty that invites us to feel superior to others. And then there is always the final word in deferred gratification, the promise of an excellent afterlife (sometimes offered as dependent on our conformity now). Not all of these are God's gifts, given in God's way. Organised religion can be self-defeating when its loud shiny rewards seduce our attention away from the greatest possible reward, which is God, living face to face with God now and forever. I find it hard to quantify what rewards an invisible God gives in this life. Our physical ears do not hear God's encouraging voice. Our heads do not feel God's reassuring pats. But these *are* there for us to discover, although we might need to find some stillness first. A calmed-down dog will appreciate a treat far more than an over excited one who snaps it out of our fingers and wolfs it down. So it is with us.

Something to chew as your dog walks alongside you
What kind of rewards do I seek from God?

HEAR THE GOSPEL
ACCORDING TO...

PSST!
STAND UP!

21

HOUSETRAINING

The dog seemed excited as I came down the stairs one morning. A minute later, I realised the word 'agitated' or 'anxious' would better describe his state. He had suffered an episode during the night and had left a large pile of mousse-like poo on the bottom step, which I discovered with a barefooted squelch as it slipped between my toes. The poor dog looked terrified. Goodness alone knows what punishments his former owners had meted out in the name of housetraining. I saw no point in telling him off. Accidents are accidents and we are all allowed to be ill. I hopped to the back door and let him rush into the garden to release anything that he was still holding in.

My dogs have always come to me as teenagers, rather than pups and as such they have been housetrained, at least to the level of relieving themselves outside. But there is more to housetraining than toileting; there are rules, such as:

- all items in the kitchen bin are off limits,
- food is only given, never stolen and
- some things are chewable whilst others are absolutely not.

HOUSETRAINING

A dog who has had more than one owner, will discover that each household has its own rules and that these are often quirky and idiosyncratic. Some owners will allow a dog to jump onto the bed, others will not.

We also need housetraining. If the Psalmist is right and we are to dwell in the house of the Lord our whole life long, then there are house rules to be learned. Jesus tells stories about God's household, in which servants continue their duties, even when God seems to be absent. Mary, the mother of Jesus, understands that in God's house the proud are humbled while the lowly are exalted, and it's the hungry who eat well, not the rich. If she is right, most of us will need considerable housetraining to unlearn society's lessons, if we are to function well under God's roof.

Churches also have their own internal house rules, and newcomers are duly housetrained to fit in. Some of these rules are taken straight from God's household, others are more ... quirky and idiosyncratic. As an inexperienced young ordinand I was invited to read the Gospel one Sunday morning. I was confused as to why the congregation remained as they were once the hymn had ended, so I invited them to be seated. The vicar whispered loudly, 'We *remain standing* for the Gospel.' In the Anglican household, I had made the rookiest of rookie errors. Other churches insist on different rules: women must cover their heads, teenagers must not wear jeans, men should shun hats unless they are bishops who get a pointy one, more properly known as a mitre. And that's another thing; churches develop their own in-house language where benches are pews, a book of services is a breviary and some (but not all) cleaning cloths are purificators. St Paul's rules included men not having long hair and women not shaving their heads.[29] And don't even mention tattoos, they have been banned since way back when.[30]

Sometimes churches insist on 'house rules' that seem counter to God, or at least God as revealed by Jesus of Nazareth. Whenever Christians find such breaches, we learn another of God's household rules, which requires us to protest, repent and reform.

---

[29] 1 Corinthians 11:6 and 14.
[30] Leviticus 19:28.

I discovered a further downside to my own church 'housetraining' when I was a prison chaplain. I met people who wanted to tell me about their encounters with God. Their unchurched words had a freshness which, whenever I attempted to quote them, I immediately dulled into 'testimonese' (a weird form of church talk). The best I could say was that they were speaking about love. And surely this is what it should boil down to, whether settling dogs into our homes or settling ourselves into God's house, all worthwhile housetraining, is all about love.

Something to chew as your dog walks alongside you
Has my religious housetraining made me a more loving person? And if not, what can I do about this?

HEY?
HOW ABOUT
THROWING THIS?
THROW IT FOR ME?
HEY?
HOW ABOUT IT?
THROW IT?
HEY?

22

FETCH!

Certain breeds have been specifically created to find things and bring them back to their humans. I'm talking about retrievers (the clue is in the name!) These dogs, belonging to the wider category of gun dogs, are bred for intelligence, gentleness and obedience: intelligence to find shot prey, gentleness to carry it without inflicting further harm and obedience to surrender it to human hunters. The American Kennel Club recognises six types, including the perennial favourite, the Labrador Retriever. They make excellent, if sometimes greedy, companions. It should be no surprise that they enjoy playing fetch.

Fetch is not always fun for humans. As with other toys, dogs seem to take an unwarranted pride in their possession of a battered, slimy tennis ball. Some humans find this 'treasure' so disgusting, that they buy plastic extensions to their arms, enabling them to keep on throwing without having to touch the horrid thing.

Some dogs love playing fetch too much. They place a stick at the feet of anyone who might throw it for them. At first there is some mutual pleasure as they joyfully hurtle off, find, collect, return and drop it, now slightly soggier and ready for a repeat. When a relentless player demands a fresh throw every five steps, a walk quickly becomes tedious.

Do we play fetch with God? What do we fetch to lay at God's

feet? In the past, we 'fetched' to God's sacred places an inordinate number of live animals, which we then slaughtered, or in sanitised language, 'sacrificed'. Sadly this practice still continues today in some parts of the world, but its popularity has been far superseded by us 'fetching' our time and our money to God. We need to be very careful that money fetched *for* God is given *to* God, by which I mean, spent to godly effect and not squandered by snake oil evangelists on private jets. As a young protestant, I was taught that God wanted me to fetch my hard work, as together we faced 'a task unfinished' of converting the world. However each Christmas we remind ourselves, that the finest thing any of us can 'fetch' seems to be …. ourselves:

> What can I give him?
> Poor as I am
> If I were a shepherd
> I would give a lamb
> If I were a wise man
> I would do my part
> Yet what I can I give him
> Give him my heart.[31]

We might struggle to imagine why the Creator of all, desires anything we little humans could fetch. And of all things, why our hearts? We might consider them unappealing: battered, chewed and broken, but to God they are a worthwhile prize. Probing further takes us deeper into an even greater mystery than why our dogs take such delight in sticks, slick with slobber.

Something to chew as your dog walks alongside you
The Quakers advise us to *fetch* or rather 'bring the whole of your life under the ordering of the spirit of Christ'.[32] Why would God want this?

---

[31] 'In the Bleak Midwinter', Christina Rossetti.
[32] Quaker *'Advice and Queries'* 1.02 – 2.

23

BE STILL!

There's an amusing moment whenever the lead and harness are lifted from their respective hooks. Most about-to-be-walked dogs will usually obstruct their attaching, not out of rebellion or mischief; quite the contrary, they are more than happy to be taken out. But their excited wriggling serves only to delay the very thing they want. And in turn, we say things like, 'Calm down you nitwit!' and 'I can't clip this onto you if you dance around like that', or more simply, 'Be still'.

It's not just walks that suffer. Have you ever needed to swat an attacking wasp away from your dog? When I tried this, the dog in question did nothing to cooperate and consequently got stung far worse than if it had stayed in one place. It yelped, it ran in circles, it howled, it bolted, none of which helped me resolve the problem. Its best path was to trust my voice and be still.

God tells us to 'be still'. Or at least the psalmist, reports God saying, 'be still and know that I am God'.[33] We need an inner stillness to worship God. When we are constantly on the move, we cannot give our best attention to God, or allow God to equip us for a task (putting on our leads and harnesses) or to protect us from worse than wasps.

[33] Psalm 46:10.

We would not want our dogs to be still too often. One of the great joys of sharing life with a dog is their rapturous welcomes. Likewise God seems to enjoy our excited dancing. King David received no rebuke from God, for his less-than-dignified jubilation when the Ark of the Covenant arrived in Jerusalem.[34] His wife, Michal may have sneered at him but God did not. When the Pharisees were alarmed by the disciples' raucous behaviour on Palm Sunday, Jesus himself confronted them and said, 'I tell you, if these were silent, the stones would shout out.'[35]

There is a time for wildness and a time for being still. We should schedule these 'still times' not just for our dogs but also for ourselves. Without them, we would miss out on so much of what God has for us, including further reasons for dancing.

 Something to chew as your dog walks alongside you
What are the fruits of true stillness?

[34]   2 Samuel 6:14.
[35]   Luke 19:40.

MUM!! HE'S GOT BETTY SUE AGAIN!

24

DROP IT!

How many of us have found ourselves saying something along these lines? 'She's got something in her mouth! What is it? Come on girl. Drop! Drop it! Good girl. Drop it. How do you make her let go? Drop it!'

'Drop it', followed by 'Leave it' are two important commands. They might not be the first we teach, but they are the ones we wish we had taught when the moment comes and we need them. It is a good idea to plan ahead and do some work with toys and sticks rather than wait for that sickening realisation that they have got hold of something valuable or dangerous. Our list of recently withheld and reluctantly surrendered items includes a receipt for something we wished to exchange, the plastic net from a bird's fat ball and a blanket that was definitely not a dog blanket.

Like our dogs, we can attach ourselves to things that do not belong to us or were only ours for a season. We also carry potentially damaging things too closely for comfort. Certainly in the West, we have a problem with possessions, but our inability to 'drop' and 'leave' is not limited to physical loads. There is emotional baggage too. Some people seem to waft through life, their burdens sitting as lightly as beads of water on a duck's back. There is much to commend about living like this, provided that care-free does not become careless. Others do not get off so lightly: worrying to the point of catastrophising, reliving past hurts, inventing better retorts for long dead arguments, reanimating redundant relationships or assuming a level of responsibility far beyond anything reasonable. It is rarely helpful when those from the first group say to those in the second, 'drop it'. Anxious people and untrained dogs find this hard to do. In truth no one actually says, 'drop it' to humans, the more common command is, 'Let it go'. And if those three words prompt a disneyfied earworm, please remember that in *Frozen*, Elsa's song 'Let it go' comes quite early on in the film and long before she is ready to drop any of her anxieties. Instead, she sings it *whilst* building a fortified, single-occupancy castle out of pure ice on a lonely mountain side. Much drama ensues before she is finally able to release her fears. The process of laying down and successfully leaving excess baggage, can be complex and painful. Often we need the kindness of others before we can begin to recognise that we might be carrying too much.

Jesus never said, 'Let it go' but he did issue commands such as 'give' (food, water, alms and so on) and 'sell' (possessions, prior to giving the money away). He tells people to 'cut off' and 'throw away' whatever causes sin, however valuable, although his specific examples (hands and eyes) were never intended to be taken literally. He also insists that we must, 'forgive'; a far wider word that encompasses 'drop it' and so much more besides. And when he said to the fishermen, 'follow', they obeyed by dropping their nets, letting go and leaving all their previous securities behind. Peter, initially the most reluctant of these, later urged others to, 'let it go,' only his actual words were, 'Cast all your anxiety on him, because he cares for you.'[36]

What does it mean today if God tells us to drop something? How do we accomplish this in practice, especially when we have been carrying an item of unnecessary baggage for far too long? If we are struggling, it might help to remember that 'drop it' is not a command that dogs instinctively welcome. They need training, support and encouragement to obey this one. And maybe we do too.

[36]   1 Peter 5:7.

Something to chew as your dog walks alongside you
Am I carrying something that I no longer need?

'NICO'

25

UNQUESTIONING OBEDIENCE

When I worked in the prison service I once watched a demonstration of the dogs and their handlers' skills. In the first exercise the dog brought down an escaping 'prisoner' (an officer dressed in padded maroon sweats). In the second the 'prisoner' turned and surrendered before the dog had reached him. The handler barked one word and the dog skidded to an immediate halt. Most dogs, running at full speed, utterly intent on their quarry, would be far too deep in the 'the Zone' to even hear, let alone obey such a command. And yet this dog stopped.

I asked earlier in this book, how would our lives look if we were so attuned to the sounds of Jesus? The answer in this context is … 'Well, this is a flawed question.' This situation is different from a previous 'chew' about listening to Jesus' every sound. Today we break the pattern of *qal wahomer*/light and heavy/'*if this is true, then how much more …*', because God does not stand over us, barking our every decision at us. We are not radio controlled robots. We are human beings, called to love God with all of our hearts, souls *and* minds. *All* of our minds. We should not expect God to micromanage our lives. Presumably God could take that level of control, but chooses not to ... at least if Jesus is a reliable guide to God. In the Gospels, Jesus silences the wind and the waves with just one command, but never attempts the same with antagonistic humans. Instead Jesus engages their minds, telling stories, offering wisdom and asking questions. When his critics stop criticising, it is because they have been stumped rather than simply told to shut up.

There are some things that we are expected to work out for ourselves. I once knew a man, let's call him 'Steve', who often skipped church on a rainy Sunday, even when he had agreed to do one of the readings. If questioned his answer ran like this, 'I was lying in bed, waiting for God to tell me it was His holy will that I should get up, but He never did. And it would be disobedient for me to act outside of God's direct instructions.' Steve, if no one else, seemed content with this logic.

God has entrusted a far larger slice of reasoning capacity to humans than to dogs. When working together, we are equipped to negotiate complex situations in ways unimaginable to any other creatures on this planet. With this greater power, comes a greater responsibility. Unquestioning obedience may be acceptable for dogs, but the nature of human obedience to God is less clear cut. Whilst it is never right for us to ignore God's orders, it is very much our duty to work out *how* we obey and also to examine *how* God's laws have been interpreted over the centuries, even to the point of asking *how* they were initially recorded. We have both the capacity and the responsibility to investigate whether we are obeying the loving God of Jesus of Nazareth and not some patriarchal construct, going by the same name. And we should also bear in mind that a tradition's longevity is by no means a failsafe guide to its godliness.

We might at times find ourselves envying our dogs; unquestioning obedience requires far less work.

 Something to chew as your dog walks alongside you
How often do I question the received wisdom of the ages?

'I ONCE WAS LOST
BUT NOW I'M FOUND'

'MAC'

26

RESTRICTIONS, LEADS AND MUZZLES

Our friends adopted a two-year-old terrier, Mac. For a while Mac responded well to training, always coming back when called. But one evening a wild scent took him deep into 'the Zone'. He ran off, his extreme focus blocking all his owners' cries. At last, at three o'clock the next morning, and after who knows what escapades, he reappeared at their door. They had long given up hunting for him, and like the father of the prodigal son, had settled to watch and wait. There was much rejoicing at both returns, but in a development on Jesus' parable, Mac found things were not quite as before. All future walks now involved a lead, admittedly a long lead. He could still run, sniff and snuffle, but never again was he accorded that former level of off-lead-trust.

How much freedom does God grant to us? Does God have a selection of leads of different lengths to control us? If we have submitted ourselves to God's guidance, might we discover certain activities are repeatedly closed-off to us, just as our dogs find themselves unable to chase sheep? Or are all restrictions something God has delegated entirely to the structures of human society?

RESTRICTIONS, LEADS AND MUZZLES

Paranoid dictators and even organised religions might hope for the latter and can leap to their perceived policing duties with alarming alacrity. If we can disentangle God from all such excessive controllings, we discover that God's desires are always for our good. All godly limits are conceived in love and delivered to us with love. But how do they work in practice?

We can (and should) debate the extent to which God might control us versus our duty to grow in self-control. How much freedom should we expect from God? As a gift, freedom can so easily be abused. One person insisting on their own unbridled freedom can severely restrict the freedoms of so many others. Imagine if we all insisted on our right to drive on whichever side of the road we chose! Reasonable external controls are necessary, even desirable.

Chaffing at every single control, restricts our enjoyment of life. Have you ever seen a dog, marching on its hind legs, choking on its lead, its front paws fruitlessly paddling at empty air while its hapless owner stumbles along behind? Their walk will become infinitely more pleasurable for both parties, once the human has trained the dog to accept certain limits. Eventually the dog will value the sense of protection that comes from being on a lead. Fair restrictions enable us all to live safely together.

It is in our nature to baulk if ever we feel unfairly controlled. I find limits easier to accept when I trust the people who set them. Politicians who consider themselves above the rules they impose on others, will never get my vote. Jesus of Nazareth seems much more trustworthy. His 'no' is only ever for our good and his ultimate desire is for the restricted to be set free.

Wouldn't we rather walk our dogs without leads? This can take a great deal of training and trust. And sadly, some dogs never reach this stage. Rehabilitating humans, from a life of offending is even more difficult; all too often society finds it easier to lock them away. But surely our desire is for all humans and all dogs to enjoy life without harming others and with no need of imposed external restrictions? That might not be attainable in every case, so in the meantime our campaigning duty is to ensure that all of society's 'muzzles and leads', from speeding fines to prison sentences, are humane, proportionate and fair, and as we are about to see, always corrective and never retaliatory.

Something to chew as your dog walks alongside you
Does God ever control me? And if so, how, when and why?

IN

JAIL

27

IN THE DOG HOUSE: CRIME AND PUNISHMENT

Imagine this scenario. On a Monday morning, you present your dog with a list of charges, relating to crimes committed in the previous week; all of which are absolutely correct. You begin the run through:

'Last Monday on your second walk you lunged when you saw a cat and very nearly pulled me over. On Wednesday you did not walk to heel at all. Then in the park on Thursday, you resolutely refused to return to me when I called you, because you were more interested in sniffing that poodle. On Friday you were a nuisance to our guests; you jumped up at them and then you begged relentlessly at the table while we were eating. On Saturday, I caught you eating fox poo. Again! And this is despite many detailed warnings, explaining why this is totally unacceptable. In view of the extreme nature of your poor behaviour, I feel I have no choice but to cut your walk times this week, remove all your toys and ban all treats.'

No sane dog owner would ever behave like this. When we need to tell our dogs off, we recognise that there is a very small window following the 'crime' in which a dog will associate their recent action with the current reproof. We have no more than a couple of seconds. Anything beyond this and a dog will fail to make that vital connection. To us humans, it might appear remorseful. We might mistake its cowering submission for an acknowledgement of its guilt. In truth it will simply be frightened. No good owner will ever punish their dog with any motive other than correction. Any talk of revenge or retaliation would be petty, as for retribution … preposterous!

Does God punish us? And if so, how? And why? There are enduring stories about the eternal fires of hell. According to these, God will confront each of us after the end of our lives with the entire catalogue of our sins, and sentence some of us to everlasting torment. But how did we end up believing God is like this? If we discipline our dogs *only* in the name of correction, surely we have to question any doctrine which says God metes out eternal punishments, beyond any hope of redemption?

Other people believe that God punishes us in this life: if we do something bad, God delivers us a slap on the wrist. Is this true? I am sure that God guides and steers us, and at times even rebukes us. If we listen, we will be aware of God's clear 'no' from time to time, but that is not the same as imagining every bad thing which comes our way must surely be God's retaliation for some earlier bad choice. I accept that if we steal, we end up in prison, if we gossip, we lose our friends, if we deliberately tell lies in public office, we will (eventually) get sacked. But I think of these more as natural consequences than as divine punishments and certainly not part of some crude system of pain-for-pain retribution. Besides, bad things can happen to us through no fault of our own. A person knocked down by a drunk driver should never be encouraged to rake through their past, seeking some forgotten sin that required their current suffering.

Walking wisely with God cannot mean walking on eggshells, forever anxious that one wrong step will unleash a thunderbolt of punitive wrath. If we do not brandish a whip at the start of each dog walk, cracking it from time to time as a reminder, why would we imagine that God is any less kind? And if, our hearts are set on correcting our dogs' behaviour rather than exacting retribution, why would we think God works the other way around with us? Perhaps we treat our dogs well because we are made in the image of a kind, wise God, and perhaps when it comes to punishment, God is like us at our absolute kindest – only much more so and with far deeper wisdom.

Something to chew as your dog walks alongside you
If we accept that God's discipline is always and only ever corrective, can we believe in an eternal hell?

28

DON'T LEAVE ME THIS WAY

Freddie was a rescued dog who could not be left alone. His history more than explains his condition. His former owner had moved house and for reasons unfathomable, had decided to leave Freddie behind, locked in an empty building without food. I am not sure how Freddie survived the days before he was found. I presume the toilet was still working and he was able to drink from there. When the door was finally knocked down, he was in a pitiful state. He was dirty, starving and distressed. These first two were quickly remedied but the distress had caused lasting damage to his mind. After a while his new owners went out for an evening, leaving him 'home alone' for the first time. When they returned they found the curtains in shreds and Freddie a quivering wreck. Nothing worked well in future attempts. They tried going out for short periods only, they left lights on and talk-radio happily chattering away, but Freddie could not cope. In the end they made the decision to reorganise their lives, so that Freddie was never left on his own again. And so it was, for the rest of his life.

Why do dogs get so anxious when left alone? One of the

answers must date back to their days as part of a wolf pack. When separated from others, some primal instinct yells from within that they cannot survive on their own and they become distressed. Once again a dog's outward appearances are deceptive: chihuahuas and papillons might not look much like wolves, but much of their brains are still wolves' brains. Most dogs seem to manage this anxiety. They get upset as we leave them, but once we are gone they settle to sleeping (or rooting through the kitchen bin). Keeping more than one dog helps to reduce their isolation anxieties, but this is not always possible.

As humans, we generally cope better than dogs with our own company, but not indefinitely. Solitary confinement can be a form of torture. We remain social animals. Like dogs, we are programmed to stay with our group. Gerard Hughes identifies, lurking behind our anxieties, our deepest fear: that of total rejection which launches us 'into the abyss of self-rejection, into nothingness and meaninglessness'.[37] If this sounds overblown, we should remember that fearing abandonment is what kept our ancestors alive. We are not the descendants of those who wandered off alone. Their genes died with them. Separation and rejection might not worry us to the same degree as our dogs, but they are nonetheless important. Gerard Hughes continues, proposing that facing this deepest fear is the route to discovering the truth about ourselves, our existence within relationships and from there, a deeper encounter with God.

Rejection is always hard. Reminding people of God's enduring love, and digging out those Bible verses about God never leaving us, might not be immediately comforting at the actual moment of break up or in the minutes after following a sacking, but ultimately that is where our consolation lies. God is the one who never dismisses us, never abandons nor forsakes us. This is why rejection by a church can be so serious. It can be hard for our minds to disentangle a welcoming God from a rejecting church, and poor treatment from the latter inevitably risks driving us from the former.

And if there is heartache, there is also rejoicing. One of the greatest benefits of owning a dog is the welcome home, especially

[37] *God of Surprises*, Gerard W. Hughes, Darton, Longman and Todd, 1985, p. 28.

after a crappy day. And if these reunions are joyful, how much more so will that great reunion be, when we finally reach our eternal home and see God face to face?

Something to chew as your dog walks alongside you
How might God help me, when facing feelings of rejection?

PART 5

ANNOYANCES

SERIOUSLY ALFIE?
YOU'VE ONLY COME IN

YEH, BUT SOMETHING
MIGHT BE HAPPENING
OUT THERE

29

IN OR OUT?

Where does your dog really want to be? All too often the answer is, 'On the other side of this closed door … please.' And then two minutes after their wish has been granted, they want to return. A dog will also sit, staring through a gate, despite having a whole garden to explore. The fascination of what might be can exert a greater draw than what actually is. If we chose to indulge our dogs' every wish, we might do little more than spend the whole day opening and closing doors for them. This game is even less fun in winter, especially when one of us is inside and the other outdoors. Our dog wants to check on both of us – 'Maybe the other one is doing something fun or has something to eat?' He has perfected the knack of operating a door handle, despite it being designed for a human hand and not a dog's paw. Sadly he displays no interest at all in learning how to close the door after him. He likes being warm, but seems oblivious to any connection between doors left open and heat leaving the house.

If to us, our dogs seem contrary, so must we to God. We often say, 'the grass is always greener on the other side'. A generation younger than mine has Katy Perry singing 'Hot N Cold'. The biblically minded might recognise within themselves that dodgy desire to return to Egypt, forsaking the promise of a new land for a familiar, if miserable life. When we are small we yearn to be older. As adults we mourn the simplicity of childhood. We fantasise about different homes, more fulfilling careers and sparkier relationships. In the midst of a sweaty, fly-raddled summer we crave bright winter days but when these come, we complain about the cold.

Christians can feel the same about Church, which on paper should be straightforward; Christians gather to worship the same God, drink from the same cup, live out the same greatest commandment and learn together from the same Bible. In reality, church life is much more complicated. We quickly discover that far from being likeminded, we often hold wildly differing opinions about God and everything else associated. Church can be the gathering where we meet the most inspiring alongside the mean-spirited. As we mature into greater self-awareness, we may discover some of these contradictions existing within ourselves. We can sit by a metaphorical closed door, imagining that beyond lies something better: a different church with warmer fellowship, more uplifting worship, fewer dull sermons and better coffee. We might even fantasise about leaving a church altogether. Sometimes, especially if we are being abused, this is the right decision. In less extreme circumstances, maybe we are like our dogs; fascinated by all that might lie beyond a closed door, whilst not valuing all that we have on this side.

But this sense of dissatisfaction, this desire to be both 'in and out', need not always be considered unholy. It is good to yearn for something beyond. St Peter tells us that we should never be fully at home in this world, but exist rather as 'aliens and exiles'.[38] St Paul looks to that ultimate 'beyond', the other side of death's door, to when we shall meet God and finally know even as we are known.[39] And at that point, we will finally lay to rest any hankering for something better.

 Something to chew as your dog walks alongside you
Am I fretting about any closed doors?

---

[38] 1 Peter 2:11.
[39] 1 Corinthians 13:12.

30
BARKING

When our dogs bark, they are telling us, 'Something's up' rather than, 'Something's wrong'.

If their barking is ever annoying, we can only blame ourselves … or if not us exactly, then certainly our ancestors. They liked their dogs to bark loudly. They slept more soundly once they had delegated all their listening-for-intruders-duties to their dogs. Dogs might spend less time howling than wolves but they more than make up for it with their barking.

Our modern dogs have yet to cotton on that their alarm-raising duties can be outsourced to electronic sensors and loudspeakers. When someone draws near to our shared territory, they let us know with an initially similar bark for friend or stranger. Their duty is to alert us (their pack) not necessarily that something is wrong, but that something is up. Often when they see us responding, they quieten down.

Of course what also might be 'up' is that they are feeling bored or lonely or in some other way distressed. This can lead to dogs barking incessantly and irritating the neighbours. In 2020 a Staffordshire man was fined near on £10,000 pounds for failing to keep his six dogs quiet. The prosecution claimed that their combined noise at times exceeded sixty decibels.

Perhaps we could think of barking as the canine equivalent of heralding. John the Baptist made a certain amount of noise when he perceived something was up, or more specifically that the Kingdom of God was at hand. His 'bark' was neither sweet nor melodious, but it did the trick of alerting the people that Someone was at the door. The Book of Acts sees Jesus' disciples barking the recent news from Jerusalem, 'Something new has happened. A man died and rose again.' St Paul's bark prompted either revival or riot, sometimes both and at the same time, as happened when he visited Ephesus.[40]

The prophets barked to warn of judgement and to give voice to the marginalised whose own bark was shouted down. We can join them, barking warnings that our planet is overheating, that inequalities are rampant, that lies proliferate and corruption multiplies; those who can make themselves heard should not stay silent. 'Something's wrong' is after all a subset of 'something's up'.

Bad things happen when good people stay silent. We have yet to work out how to bark wisely and effectively. Yapping angrily on Twitter might be a start, but it is not enough, and there are some major pitfalls. Now, as when Jesus walked the earth, the powerful are good at silencing any barking that gets too irritating: by blocking their ears, by trivialising the barkers or by more violent methods. But we have a holy duty to bark and continue barking. If we are struggling to know where to start, we could consider John the Baptist's bark, 'Make straight the way of the Lord'[41] or even St Paul's, 'now is the day of salvation'.[42]

Something's up! God's rule is dawning! Good news for the downtrodden! God is love!

Something to chew as your dog walks alongside you
Are there times when I could make more noise?

---

[40] Acts 19.
[41] John 1:23.
[42] 2 Corinthians 6:2.

31

HOWLING

Our childhood dog would join me as I practised my clarinet, throwing back his head and adding an only slightly less tuneful accompaniment. Only once did a later dog let out a low, mournful howl. It was just after I'd turned off the light, on his first night in my home. This remained a one off. Domestic dogs rarely howl.

In contrast, wolves howl a great deal. If barking is an alert, 'something's up', howling is their way of saying, 'Here I am. Where are you?'. A howl travels a long distance. It gathers the pack together, from all corners of its wide territory. The howl of the leader, says, 'Come and join me!' The rest of the family howl their response, 'I'm here. On my way!' Lone wolves, exiled from their pack do not join in at these times, but might howl when it is quieter, to attract others like themselves to form a new pack. We will never know all their reasons for howling, but these are enough to explain why one dog sang along with my clarinet and another, newly removed from a crowded shelter, wanted to know if there were any fellow dogs nearby.

We likewise want to know where our loved ones are. We do not howl, but we visit, phone and text each other. When lonely or settling into a new place, we seek out kindred spirits. We say,

'Birds of a feather flock together' but we could have equally chosen a lupine aphorism: Leon Trotsky once said, 'When one runs with the wolves, one must howl with the pack.'

God's work on earth will not be accomplished by individuals working alone. Christians believe we are called to live as a pack, although we would more usually say 'family' or Church. Church at its best, resounds with the wolfish howls of its members, checking in with one another and meeting regularly for communal howling. Sometimes a wolf will set up a howl which gathers the likeminded to add their voices. Wilberforce did not defeat slavery by working alone. Rosa Parks' defiance rallied many more in Montgomery, Alabama to boycott the buses until Black people could sit wherever they wanted.

In the previous reading, I said that bad things happen when good people stay silent. Today I will add: communal howling is better than lone barking and good things happen when good people rally together. We could benefit from being more wolf-like and howling together more often, if that meant more networking, more cooperation, more checking-in with each other and more following of decent leads from decent leaders.

Something to chew as your dog walks alongside you
Whose current howl inspires me to howl along with them?

32
PEEING

'**D**o you have to pee on everything?' I ask in frustration as he interrupts our walk … again! I might be in a hurry, there may be storm clouds brewing overhead, but whenever the dog wants to pee, he slams on the brakes.

Every Friday morning, I used to collect the latest edition of the *Church Times* while walking my then dog. The newsagent owned a couple of dogs, who seemed to live permanently under the shop's glass-fronted counter. They were always interested to see my dog, who likewise returned their friendly wags. One Friday my dog looked for them, saw they were out and, before I could stop him, left a calling card … which is to say he lifted his leg and peed on something they would notice. It was a box of Walkers Ready Salted. I would have felt better if the newsagent had allowed me to buy it, but he just smiled, shrugged and said, 'Dogs! What can you do?'

Why do dogs need to pee so often? The most frequent answer is that they are marking out their territory. It is also likely that the rich combination of scents contains a variety of information for those with noses to smell, possibly signalling among other things, the pee-er's social status and fertility.

Unfortunately what is common sense to our canine

companions, is all rather disgusting to us humans. But flipping this around, I wonder how God views *our* current methods of advertising our presence and sharing our information. We make these marks not by micturating, but by posturing and incessant chatter. Recently we have discovered an unprecedented boost to our range via the internet. Whatever did we do in previous millennia with the extra time we now dedicate to Facebook? How many tweets boil down to the appeal, 'Validate me and my views'? And is this good for us? We certainly get dopamine hits from seeing a large number of 'likes' on our posts but there is a downside. Instagram has been singled out for damaging young people's mental health,[43] but it is hardly alone.

Some dogs will pee on the exact same spot where another has just peed. This is an act of dominance: a superior asserting their status over an inferior, drowning out one set of messages with a torrent of their own. Provided this is done outside, it is far less disturbing than our human habits of trolling, cyberbullying, catfishing, piling on, doxxing and generally harassing those who dare to post something we do not like.

And perhaps God wonders why we prefer validation from strangers over real encounters with friends and family. A cartoon: a man in pyjamas is typing feverishly, wide eyes fixed on his screen. A husky speech bubble floats from a bedroom door (open wide enough to reveal a pair of seductive legs): 'Come to bed darling and play with me.' The man replies: 'In a minute! There's someone on the internet who is WRONG!'

I imagine God finds some of our internet habits even less appealing than we would find a urine-soaked box of crisps?

 Something to chew as your dog walks alongside you
If we get grossed out by some of our dogs' territorial behaviour, what does God make of ours?

---

[43] 'Facebook Knows Instagram is Toxic for Teen Girls, Company Documents Show', *Wall Street Journal*, Georgia Wells, Jeff Horwitz and Deepa Seetharaman 14-09-2021

SHEEEESHHH!

33

BEGGING AND DIGNITY

'What on earth is he doing?' we asked each other. Within a few days of arriving in our home, our rescued two-year-old started exhibiting some rather peculiar behaviour. Whenever one of us had a biscuit, he placed both paws on our knees and then leant back onto his haunches until his spine was almost vertical, all the while holding a rather vacant expression on his face. He did this several times before it dawned on us that his previous owners had taught him to beg. Presumably they thought he looked cute. To us, he looked both uncomfortable and demeaned. It is bad enough with smaller dogs but our great lunk looked plain ridiculous. I recalled how once, as a small child, I had seen performing dogs in a circus. One, dressed as an Edwardian nanny, walked on its hind legs while pushing a pram. Even then, I failed to see anything appealing. And just note, wolves never feature on any circus bill. They refuse to be so coerced.

I am not against dogs performing. I love watching well-trained dogs being put through their paces, negotiating an obstacle course. Unlike the poor beasts in the circus, these ones are clearly happy. They are dogs beings dogs, not being forced to act as mini humans (and I shudder to imagine how much cruelty is involved in training a dog to push a pram).

The begging itself is bad enough. Mealtimes are no fun accompanied by a slobbering dog, eyes fixed on my next mouthful. Well-fed, well-cared-for dogs have no need to beg. Feeding them scraps from the table sends them confusing messages and encourages them to pester.

I do not believe that God wants us to beg. Jesus teaches us to ask, seek and knock, to simply present our requests to a God, who requires no song and dance, no further cajoling or additional persuasion to listen to us. We are to approach God as we would a loving parent, trusting that no needful thing will be withheld from us. It's one of Jesus' best known 'qal wahomer' sayings:

'If you then, who are evil, know how to give good gifts to your children, how much more will your Father in heaven give good things to those who ask him!'[44]

God accords us human dignity. Begging falls beneath that level. Failing human societies might force humans to beg, but God never does. And our dogs are doubtless happier once they have learnt that begging is pointless, since they are given all they need at their own mealtimes. Our dog soon gave up sitting up on his haunches. Of course he's still interested in our food. I doubt that will ever stop, but at least he no longer demeans himself by begging.

 Something to chew as your dog walks alongside you
Have I ever felt the need to beg from God?

---

44 Matthew 7:11.

'PERFECT LOVE CASTS OUT FEAR.'

'TOSCA & MIMI'

34

BITING AND HEALING

My friend Anne adopted two small sisters and with a musical flourish, named them Mimi and Tosca. In their early lives, they had more contact with concrete than with humans, having been kept caged in a barn. As a consequence, they had little idea of how to behave in a warm home. The initial messes and puddles were less of an issue: the real worry was their aggression, especially after one visitor had hobbled home, nursing a bitten ankle.

By the time I met these two sisters, they were only delightful. As I sat down, first Tosca then Mimi leapt onto my lap, both settling quickly and falling asleep as if they had known me for years. How does such a transformation occur? The answer is slowly and lovingly. Anne's love bought them constant reassurance and in time, they let go of their fears. Their aggression was only ever the presenting issue, behind it lay the real problem – they were frightened. This, combined with the inherent feistiness of their breed, manifested in biting.

Some dogs never fully recover from early trauma. These two certainly have. They understand that they no longer need aggression to survive. Now whenever alarmed, they crouch down and wait to be picked up. Their trust in the safety of their owner's arms, is total.

Apparently the Bible records 365 versions of the phrase, 'Do not be afraid' (although if I were a shepherd, scared witless by an angel I might retort, 'OK, but how about - do not explode in a burst of light right in front of my nose in the middle of the night?') If anger and aggression truly are secondary symptoms of the real malaise, fear, it would make sense to make fear the target of our therapies. Like dogs, we humans can be scarred deeply by traumatic events. There is no one fix for all. The PTSD specialist, Bessel van de Kolk recommends several treatments, one of which is stroking a pet. The combination of a repetitive action and a warm living being, can soothe those parts of the brain which flare up all too quickly in PTSD sufferers.[45] There are also successful rehabilitation programmes, which pair rescued dogs with so-called 'hopeless' prisoners. Dogs can find a way in, bypassing fears and scars and thus locating the deeply buried humanity present in even the worst offenders.[46] I doubt any of this is news to God. God sees beyond our bad behaviour to the wounds that lie beneath. There is a pleasing sense of wonder, when God's healing for humans is part and parcel of God's healing for dogs.

St John teaches us (and we can surely extend this to our dogs) 'There is no fear in love, but perfect love casts out fear.'[47]

 Something to chew as your dog walks alongside you
Are there any fears that I carry needlessly? And if so, how might God help me?

---

[45] *The Body Keeps The Score*, Bessel Van Der Kolk, Penguin, 2014.
[46] 'Pets in prison: the rescue dogs teaching Californian inmates trust and responsibility', Hilda Burke, The *Observer*, 19 Apr 2020.
[47] 1 John 4:18.

35

MUDDY PAWS

Vincent van Gogh found himself in that awkward position of being an adult back under his parents' roof and under their rules. He had had a girlfriend and they had lived independently. But when the relationship broke down, he had nowhere else to go and so he returned to his parents. They took him in because he was their son. He stayed because he had no better option. It was a tense time all round. Vincent chafed at their strictures and in a letter to his brother Theo, described himself as being as welcome as a large sheepdog. He imagines his parents complaining:

'He will come into the living room with muddy paws – and also, he is just too shaggy. He will get in everyone's way and his bark is so loud. Let's just say it, he's a dirty beast.'[48]

He continues:

'So this home is too good for me, and Pa and Ma and the family present such a genteel facade (not underpinned by genuine feelings however) and – and there are clergy, many clergy. The dog understands that if he stays, it will be too much for them to endure, and his being 'in this house' would be barely tolerated, so he plans to find himself an actual dog-house elsewhere.'

[48]   Vincent van Gogh, Letter 346 (413), to Theo 15/12/1883.

Those of us who own dogs know that newly cleaned floors do not stay pristine for long. Piles of hair (surely bigger than the actual dog!) quickly accumulate in corners. And why, after a walk in the rain, will they only do their proper full-body-shake once they are indoors? Those who get very stressed about such things, might be better off with a goldfish. The rest of us accept a bit of mud as part and parcel of the great joy of living with a canine companion.

The phrase 'muddy paws' does not feature in any translation of the Bible that I can find. But if God is anything like the prodigal son's father, then ragged clothes, a scruffy demeanour and a certain piggy whiff present no barrier to a welcome home hug.

If you belong to a church, does it welcome 'shaggy sheepdogs'? For all the talk of love, they get the message whenever they are not welcome. And all of us at times are misfits, bounding around, leaving muddy paw prints across God's world. If God can cope, God's Church has no business minding too much. All healthy churches will have their own collection of much loved shaggy sheepdogs. Sometimes some behaviour *does* need challenging, but this can be done with kindness and tact. There are good ways of drawing lines and cleaning up, which do not leave the muddy-pawed feeling diminished. Unhealthy churches leave God's beloved eccentrics feeling as van Gogh did at the end of his analogy.

'The dog has just one regret, which is that he didn't stay away; he wasn't as lonely out there on the heath as he is here in this house – despite the good intentions.'

 Something to chew as your dog walks alongside you
Have you ever been treated as an unwelcome shaggy sheepdog? How well do you cope when others walk with muddy paws through your life?

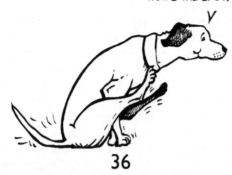

GAAAHHH!!!
LOOK WHAT SHE'S DOING
ON THE AXMINSTER

OOO YEH!
THAT'S THE SPOT!

36

OTHER 'DISGUSTING' THINGS THAT DOGS DO

The schoolboy in me clamoured to include this section. My 'inner parent' strongly advised caution while the 'adult me' rolled his eyes. The schoolboy won and I gleefully drew up a list a disgusting things dogs do: sniffing each other's bottoms, humping human legs, rolling in filth, dragging their itchy rear ends across the floor, displaying inopportune lipsticks and of course eating other animals' poo ... I could go on but my inner parent is now looking decidedly tetchy ...

I once played my guitar with freezing fingers for an Easter morning ecumenical 'sunrise' service. The sun did rise, but without any of the drama of Jesus bursting from the tomb. It was thickly veiled by a blanket of grey clouds. The Baptist preacher did his level best to penetrate the gloom but his endeavours were hampered not just by the chilling drizzle but also by my friend's dog, who had crept behind him to pursue a primal instinct with the vicar's collie. My inner parent had quite the battle with my inner child that morning.

Dogs have many physiological differences from us. One

is fundamental. A richly smelling bottom is social suicide for a human. It quite the opposite for a dog. It is more than desirable, it is designed. They have evolved to communicate with each other via scent, and their most important scent secreting glands are located in small sacs on either side of their anuses. It is entirely natural for them, on meeting another member of their species, to direct their noses towards the very last place we would wish to visit with ours. When the openings to these sacs become blocked, they free them by scooting their rears across our carpets. We might want to reason with our dogs about when is and isn't an appropriate time for a variety of things. These are not battles we will easily win. Most of the time we are requiring them to stop being dogs to spare us from human embarrassment. Perhaps we should resign ourselves to chuckling along with the children?

There are other primal instincts that we do have a duty to curb. Our dogs may have inherited hunting instincts from their wolf ancestors but we cannot allow them to harass farm animals. We can also lament when foxes, their not-so-distant cousins, kill every bird in the coop. Not all disgusting behaviour has a funny side.

But if we find certain canine habits revolting, what does God make of our antics? How does God react to those human actions, which we *as humans* call sickening? We can do things which far surpass a fox's greedy destruction. In the Harry Potter books, the headteacher, Albus Dumbledore acknowledges that, being cleverer than most, his mistakes can be larger.[49] Humans, being cleverer than foxes have a wider reach and being far better organised, get to misbehave on a far grander scale. Foxes, wolves and dogs will not have to answer for the Climate Emergency, rights abuses, rampant inequality, polluting the oceans with plastic, industrialised factory farming and species extinction. Our cleverer human brains are behind all these issues and we stand accountable. Maybe, collectively, we can solve them. God, if asked, will no doubt guide us but as previously observed, God will not bark the solutions at us.

And yet despite our wanton damage to Creation, God does not view us with disgust. Maybe God remembers that we too are

[49] *Harry Potter and the Half-Blood Prince*, J. K. Rowling, Bloomsbury, 2003.

still animals, no matter how evolved we imagine we are. God looks at us with love. One of the great mysteries of Christianity is how God sees all our misdeeds and yet continues to love us.

 Something to chew as your dog walks alongside you
What level of collective action is required to heal the world? What responsibility falls to us as humans and what belongs to God?

PART 6

A DOG'S LIFE

37

PERPETUAL PUPPIES

It would take a very hard hearted human not to be moved on meeting a puppy. Everything about puppies is delightful: their uncoordinated movements, their playfulness, their fascination with the world around and their ability to fall asleep anywhere, even as they are eating. Well, not *everything* is delightful; the chewed shoes, the widdles and unexpected poos are all tiresome, but most of us find these very easy to forgive. I find puppies especially endearing in those brief moments when they try to act with the full dignity of an adult dog before collapsing back into ridiculousness.

Puppydom continues: our dogs remain as perpetual adolescents throughout their lives. This is quite deliberate. We keep them dependent on us, never allowing them to reach the full maturity of a breeding wolf in the wild. As our pups grow up they might lose some of their clumsy cuteness, but they retain their puppyish core. This is part of their appeal to grown up humans. They become our bridge to a happier state. As infants we shared their transparent emotions; we could be completely joyful or utterly devastated with a purity of feeling, no longer unavailable to us as adults. On Christmas Eve, parents of a six-year-old might catch something of their own former rapture, along with the wistful reminder that they will never again experience such unalloyed excitement. The perpetual puppy inside a dog of any age also connects us to those less nuanced days.

If I say dogs have pure thoughts, by 'pure' I mean 'undiluted' rather than radiant goodness, sweetness and light. When they want something, it seems to fill their minds entirely. When they are happy, their happiness is everything, and the same goes for being sad or frightened. I am not sure how often we can talk of dogs experiencing mixed feelings; when faced with a choice of emotions, they seem to flit, rapidly abandoning one in order to fully commit to another, rather than holding several in balance. There was a wolf in Narnia, who wanted to attack a child, but was so angry he had to first stop and howl.[50]

God does not keep us as perpetual babies. We are expected to grow up (more on this soon) but never to the point where we have outgrown God. Some adults call their parents by their first names. Jesus never envisaged his followers reaching an equivalent stage with God. There is no provision in the Lord's Prayer for anything beyond 'Abba' or 'Daddy'. We have changed this into the rather sober 'Our Father' and in the process, eroded the implicit childlike dependence. I am sure that Mum, Mam, Mom, Mama or Imma are also more than acceptable. After all, King David likened his relationship with God, to a child being soothed by his Mum, encouraging all God's people to seek the same intimacy:

> O Lord, my heart is not lifted up, my eyes are not raised too
> high;
> I do not occupy myself with things too great and too
> marvellous for me.
> But I have calmed and quieted my soul, like a weaned child
> with its mother;
> my soul is like the weaned child that is with me.
> O Israel, hope in the Lord from this time on and for
> evermore.

> (Psalm 131)

Note how David stresses that he is not a baby. He is older – weaned – old enough to seek out his Mum's company, knowing that she is his

[50]   *The Lion, the Witch and the Wardrobe*, C. S. Lewis, 1950.

peace-filled refuge. I often think of this Psalm in the evenings when our dog is sprawled asleep across both of our laps, with the pure trust of one who feels safe and loved. Is David right? Does God invite all of us to share this same security?

And I was wrong earlier on, when I said that as adults, we will never know unadulterated joy again. A day will come when we see God face to face. At that homecoming the purity of our rejoicing shall surpass that of our puppies' *and* our six-year-old Christmas Eve selves.

Something to chew as your dog walks alongside you
Could I ever have such a childlike trust in God, that it would rival my dog's puppyish trust in me?

38

ADOPTION – HOW IT USUALLY BEGINS FOR US

Our dogs join our lives by adoption, unless we're lucky enough to have puppies born in our home. Sometimes this adoption is planned: a visit to a breeder or to a rescue centre. Sometimes it just happens.

My friend Matt had wanted a dog for a long time. His wife, Jo was vocally less keen. She reasoned that she already had three children getting under her feet (their two youngsters … and Matt). Why would she want a dog too?

Early one morning Matt heard some strange sounds coming from outside their front door: a scuffling and was that also a quiet whimpering? On opening he found a small brown dog that he had never seen before. She was frightened, she was cold, but despite whatever cruelties she had known, she still wanted to trust humans. At some point in the night she must have decided that behind this door, she would find friendly people. Matt knelt down and she allowed herself to be picked up.

And then, with more than a degree of trepidation, he took her into the kitchen. Jo looked up and saw what he was carrying.

'Love at first sight' cannot easily be explained. And Jo might still refute that she had ever felt anything so soppy, but it was she who did the adoption research and discovered that the poor dog would have to be in a pound for seven days. And it was she, who phoned in every day, anxiously checking to see if any former owners had identified themselves. And at the end of the longest week (in which the children had named the dog Chewie) it was she who bought her home and into the family.

St Paul wrote that each of us undergoes our own version of this story, with God.[51] When we come to faith, we join God's family and receive a spirit of adoption, by whom we cry, 'Abba! Father!'. I like the phrase, 'God has no grandchildren'. We are adopted directly by God, who gives us exactly the same titles and privileges as if blood heirs, born into the family. I don't know why St Paul also tells the Christians in Corinth that he, Paul, is their father and they are his children.[52] That seems like a tragic unravelling of his great theme of adoption.

But leaving St Paul to one side; if we can find a space in our hearts and homes to make a stray mutt a full family member, then how much more will God, who is love, joyfully make room for us?

Something to chew as your dog walks alongside you
How long does it take a dog to settle into its new home and how long for us to accept deep down, that we are truly God's beloved children?

Also … anyone considering buying a puppy should follow the guidance on the RSPCA website and thus avoid funding illegal puppy farms. Search www.rspca. org.uk for 'Buying a Puppy'.

---

[51] Romans 8:15.
[52] I Corinthians 4:14-15.

39

GROWING OLDER –
THE JOURNEY FROM
PUP-P TO OA-P

It is remarkable how dogs can stay puppyish all the way into old age ... mentally that is, sadly not physically. A walk that was once a breeze suddenly becomes a slog and then, an impossibility. Trips to the vet, along with visits to the garden become more regular, and hiding pills in food, part of the daily routine.

The truth is unavoidable: dogs have shorter lifespans than humans and consequently they age much more quickly. A young pup, bursting with life looks invincible. We might even look forward to future days when they have a bit less bounce. And yet all too quickly we notice them struggling to rise. As with us, they grow grumpier and less tolerant of over-enthusiastic pups (both canine and human).

We have to adapt and make decisions they will not always understand. Again we find ourselves trying to reason with them, 'I'm sorry lovely. It's best for you to stay home in the warm. We are going out for a while, and where we're going, there'll be a lot of walking and you won't like it.' That puppyish excitement around going out, never fully disappears.

We make adjustments for our ageing dogs and surely God does the same for us. Old age should not be viewed with sadness, whether it is us or our dogs who are getting on a bit. There is much to enjoyed at every stage of life and each season brings its own rewards. Dogs seem to spend more time sleeping by radiators, or when available, in pools of sunlight. Some humans complain endlessly, but others seek the new benefits. In retirement, the alarm clock heralds a gentle start to a new day, not the former mad rush to get washed, fed and out of the door.

Our relationship with God (and with ourselves) moves into new territories as we mature. Gerard Hughes proposes that there are three stages in our walk with God, infancy, adolescence and adulthood: the institutional (everything is done for us), the critical (we question everything) and the mystical (we explore much more deeply). He argues that we need all three and that moving to the next stage must not eradicate the previous. But it is in the adult/mystical stage that we truly encounter the God of Surprises, whilst we engage with the layers upon layers of complexity within us. The process is both troubling and compelling. It repels as it attracts or in the phrase of certain mystics, it is a mystery '*tremendum et fascinans*'. Naturally he says this far better than I do here in my briefest of summaries and I wholeheartedly recommend his book, as invaluable to anyone wishing to grow in God.[53] The key message is that growing older is no bad thing for human or dog, as long as we never lose touch with our inner puppy, and we keep bringing ourselves back to God.

 Something to chew as your dog walks alongside you
Quakers encourage each other to, 'Approach old age with courage and hope'.[54] What might this look like in my everyday life?

---

[53] *God of Surprises,* Gerard W. Hughes, Darton, Longman and Todd, 1985 (see chapter 2, 'Clearing the Approaches').
[54] Quaker '*Advice and Queries*' 1.02 – 29

40

AT THE END

I watched as my elderly dog walked creakily out onto a sunlit lawn. He gently lowered himself down, toppling a bit towards the finish but no damage was done, the warm ground was soft and he was soon asleep. His days of boundless energy were gone. Walks were now limited to an exploration of the garden. He no longer minded when I left the house without him and my welcome home was often a single whump of his tail on the carpet. He was tired. He showed no signs of being ill. He was just old. And as I looked at him lying on the grass, I suddenly wished that his long sleep would begin there and then.

I knew his death was coming. If I am honest, my prayer that day was more for me, than him; I so dreaded making *the* choice that he could not make for himself. He carried on into the autumn. A friend told me, that I would know the day when it finally came. And I did. One morning he staggered into my study and as he tried to settle, he collapsed and yelped with pain. And I knew. I knew as I helped him into the car, that this would be our last ride together. I knew, before the vet discovered an inoperable tumour in his abdomen. I knew.

I stayed with him. Some people choose not to, but I refused to imagine it any other way. He had been alongside me for so long and through so much. I had to be with him. This was the last thing I could do for him. Everything that followed: the collection of his body, his cremation and the scattering of his ashes – these were for me, not him. I held him, his head on my lap until I was sure that he had breathed his last. And then, for the first time in thirteen years, I had no idea where he was. He was my companion no more.

The sadness felt unbearable. Most people were very kind. A few said, 'Oh come on, it was only a dog', or worse, 'Why not get another?' My Mum said, 'It's a very pure grief, when we grieve for a dog.' I looked confused and so she explained, 'We have no history of strife with a dog and so our love is purer. Their love for us is of course pure because it is unconditional. And so we find our grief for a dog is also pure, often sharper and cleaner than other griefs.' She was right. We need to treat this wound with care, ignoring the remarks of those who cannot comprehend. We need time. And I believe we act unfairly if we rush too quickly to adopt another. How can we be ready to meet it as a new being, and not just as a replacement?

If we feel such pain at these partings, can we talk about God ever feeling anything akin? And if so, how, when and why? Jesus was so moved at the sight of the grief-stricken, that he joined his tears with theirs.[55] Can we contemplate God being likewise affected, when grief for our beloved dogs howls within us?

 Something to chew as your dog walks alongside you
How astonishing is the shortest verse in the Bible, 'Jesus wept'?

---

[55] John 11:35.

PART 7

DOGS AND PRAYER

THE GAZE OF LOVE

41

TALKING NONSENSE AND CRINKLING EARS

Our spoken words to our dogs are rarely well thought through. We are repetitive at best. Mostly we talk utter nonsense, in voices pitched a notch or two higher than normal. Just listen to yourself, the next time you fuss your dog. And then imagine that a work colleague or someone you are keen to impress, is eavesdropping. Few of us want to be overheard saying:

'Who's got *floppy* ears then? *Who's* got floppy ears then? *You've* got floppy ears! Haven't you? Haven't *you* got floppy ears? Haven't you just got the *snoogiest, zoogiest, floppiest* ears ever? *Yes* you have!'

It falls some distance short of the carefully crafted eloquence of say, Barack Obama. Nevertheless, this is exactly the kind of babble we spout to our dogs on a daily basis. So why do we do it? The simplest answer is that our dogs condition us. When we behave like this, they reward us. They give us their waggling tails and snuffling noses. And the more we make excitable, squeaky sounds, the more attention they give to us. So we carry on, at least until we suspect that someone else might be listening in.

And if this is how we behave towards our dogs, then how much more does God, who loves us with an even greater love, behave towards us? Relax! I'm not going to suggest that God ever speaks to us in baby talk. However I suspect that the original source of all those good emotions, however inanely we express them, is to be found in God. Sister Wendy Beckett calls this, 'the Gaze of Love'. It is the harmony of warm admiration and boundless joy, so high, deep and wide that our best experiences of it in this life, are but mere glimpses. If the sight of our dogs awakens in us such pleasure, how much more does God delight in us?

Maybe this is why St John for almost two millennia, has been encouraging us to rejoice:

'See what love the Father has given us, that we should be called children of God; and that is what we are.'[56]

I am convinced that churches would be far happier places and by consequence far more attractive to newcomers, if we as Christians spent more time basking in God's gaze of love, just as our dogs love the fuss we make of them.

 Something to chew as your dog walks alongside you
Can I ever imagine God crinkling my ears?

SO HOW ABOUT A WALK?
OR MAYBE SOME FOOD?
WALK? FOOD? WALK?

R. I. P.
Tobermory

42

WHAT IF OUR DOGS COULD TALK BACK...?

At the start of this book I asked about how best I could talk to my dog. But what if he could talk back to me? That would be fun … wouldn't it? Or maybe not? Hector Hugh Munro, better known as Saki, once wrote a short story about a cat who had been given the gift of speech. His name was Tobermory. He caused mayhem in the refined human circles around and above him, by repeating overheard conversations to those who were being talked about, rather than talked to. The humans became distressed. Tobermory suddenly vanished and his disappearance was mourned by no one.

We sometimes imagine a life in which our pets really could speak to us. In these fantasies, they become fully anthropomorphised beings: agony aunts, best mates, sages and seers full of wise perspectives and warm reassurances. The reality might be far more mundane. If dogs had speech, would their conversational range be riveting?

'Want food. Want mate. Want play. Want walk. Want tummy rub. Food yippee! Walkies yippee! Noooooo – don't leave me! You're back – yippee! Want food. Want mate. Want play.' Etc.

Quite possibly I am being grossly unfair to our canine companions, but if I am right, we would soon tire of their chatter and wish they would return to their former speechless states.

Turning all this around, we remember that God *has* given the gift of speech to us humans, and even more generously has promised a listening ear to all who pray in faith. If we sometimes want our dogs to speak, how much more does God want to hear our words? But what if, in God's ears, our conversational range is only marginally less banal than that of our dogs? We repeat the same petty worries day after day. We trot out familiar set formulae, sometimes neglecting to even listen to ourselves as we speak. In public worship, we pray things out loud which we might not wholeheartedly believe but nevertheless make us sound good. We allow ourselves to be utterly distracted halfway through praying something important. We mix the grand with the trivial; we can fret about the climate *and* ask for a parking space for our 4x4 in pretty much the same breath. And yet the wonder, mystery and joy of prayer is that God chooses to keep on listening to us. Over-practised eloquence, tact and delicacy are positively discouraged, if they disrupt our saying what really matters. God seems to prefer our issues to be surrendered, freshly dug from the mine of our hearts, no matter how rough, uncut, unpolished or poorly phrased they are. To have our words so valued is an immense privilege.

I have been far too cynical about our dogs. They are talking to us all the time, but being dogs, they express themselves in a variety of ways, none of which are akin to our preferred human method. And I am sure that, if given the power of speech, they would tell us that they love us. They might even thank us. And we too do well if sometimes we break the repetitive litany of our needs to offer the same to God.

 Something to chew as your dog walks alongside you
How much thought should we put into how we talk to God?

43

DO DOGS PRAY?

Is there a separate god for dogs? OK I know what the answer is, or at least what it be should be for any well-schooled Christian, Muslim or Jew. So why am I bothering to ask the question? It is prompted by a line in the film, *Fried Green Tomatoes at the Whistlestop Café* Ruth passes on to Idgie, her Momma's view that there is a separate god for children. This notion left me a tad discombobulated. Why was such a god needed? And what would he, or she be like? The story is set in Alabama, in the deep South, in what we would now call the Bible Belt, not exactly fertile ground for polytheism. On first hearing it, my monotheism-saturated soul baulked, 'This is nonsense! There's one God! Only one! For all of us, adults and children alike!'

But maybe Ruth's Momma associated 'God' more with preaching, hierarchy, respectability, frowning and starch ... and less with the things a child needs: nurture, encouragement, kindness and understanding. So if 'God' did not provide these and yet someone clearly watched over children, it follows that somewhere out there, there must be 'a separate god for children'.

What would a separate god for dogs look like? Human history offers some ideas. The ancient Egyptians and the Aztecs both had versions of a canine headed human, Anubis and Xolotl. Gula, Bau or

Nintinugga were all names for a Babylonian goddess, who stories and images (and consequently temples) were filled with dogs. The Indigenous people of North America had Coyote. Greek Hecate often had a dog's body and sometimes one of her three heads was a dog's. Searching for an answer to my own question took me far away to the Russian steppes, where I imagined a wise old she-wolf, revered as The Great Mother, even by the subspecies bred from her immediate children.

Surely the answer is not to imagine a pantheon, but to expand our view of God and ditch the long-haired old man sitting on a cloud? There is a God for dogs, but not a separate one from ours. The God for humans is the same being. The problem is that we humans who claim to know God, often act as if God is ours and ours alone. But Jesus warned us away from this, by telling us that each falling sparrow is noted by God. Why should we imagine that the same God fails to notice each caged, chained, lonely and abused dog? Maybe if we believed in a 'separate god for dogs' we might treat dogs better?

Dogs are God's wonderfully made creatures. How does God view our treatment of them? An artist's work always remains important to them. How would Rembrandt react if we left his paintings out in the rain? How much more should we care for all of God's carefully designed animals? This leads us beyond humans and dogs and towards the unsettling definitions of 'pet or plate'. Cows, octopuses, horses, sheep, pigs, herring, goats, turtles, chickens and ducks are also God's creatures. They do not have their own separate gods. Their God is also our God. So how does our shared God view our brutal factory farms, our methods of slaughter, our rape of the oceans … combined with our scandalous waste of food?

We'll never know if dogs have any concept of their Creator. An old hymn states that all animals worship their maker:

'The humbler creation, though feeble their lays,
With true adoration, shall sing to Thy praise!'[57]

---

[57] 'O Worship the King all glorious above', Robert Grant (1833).

DO DOGS PRAY?

What might this look like in practice? I am deeply touched when I read how Rabbi Jonathan Wittenberg sometimes prays, covering both himself and his collie, Mitzpah with his shawl. He does this on days when he is struggling to focus and he wonders if his dog, perhaps without even being conscious of the act, prays more deeply, more naturally and with his entire being, to their shared God.[58]

Something to chew as your dog walks alongside you
How might *my* dog approach our shared God?

---

[58] *Things My Dog Has Taught Me About Being a Better Human*, Jonathan Wittenberg, Hodder & Stoughton, 2017, pp. 62-64.

OOO YUM! FOOD!

OH DANG! IT'S THAT DARN BELL!

AGAIN!

44

PAVLOV'S DOGS – OUR NEED OF RITUAL

Feeding time is an insanely exciting moment in any dog's day. As it draws near, they become increasingly alert. They jump up the moment we rise from a chair. They follow us wherever we go. They position themselves directly in our paths. In short they do everything within their power to remind us of their hunger and of our duties.

Ivan Pavlov observed the dogs in his laboratory starting to salivate at the mere arrival of their feeder. He decided to ring a bell at the moment when the feeder arrived. After a while, the sound of the bell alone was enough to prompt his dogs to drool. This is called classical conditioning, respondent conditioning and also, in honour of the man himself, pavlovian conditioning. I wonder how he would feel about posterity's decision to forever after associate his name with dog slobber? He should feel honoured, humbled ... and deeply ashamed ... because he was extremely cruel to the dogs in his care.[59]

Do we as humans have pavlovian responses to God? I believe

[59] *Our Dogs, Ourselves*, Alexandra Horowitz, Simon & Schuster, 2019, pp. 10-11.

we do and moreover, that we initiate these for ourselves. We have all sorts of routines to awaken our hunger for God's presence. The call of the muezzin brings Muslims to prayer. Christians have hymns in which the singer and not God, is the principal addressee: 'Praise *my soul* the King of Heaven', '*Come*, now is the time to worship', 'Be still *my soul*' and so on. We ring such bells, along with more literal ones, to prepare ourselves for worship.

Dogs also follow certain rituals. Early on we established a feeding routine, which requires our boy to sit and wait for permission before starting to eat. All ran smoothly for a while, but then he started playing up. Why would he do this? We looked at our own behaviour and found the answer. A minor injury had temporarily suspended me from dog walking. My husband had stepped up and taken over. To compensate I had decided to prepare the dog's food ahead of their return. It was then that he had started to act up. He was confused by the missing rituals: the collecting of the bowl, the move to the cupboard, the rustling of bags, the crank of the tin opener and the release of those enticing aromas. All his usual prompts were missing and he didn't know what to do.

Our praying likewise benefits from a variety of prompts. Sometimes circumstance demand that we just start but in the normal run of things, we do well to begin our prayer times gently, as a singer warms up their voice or an athlete goes through their stretching exercises. These prompts will be different for each of us. We need to find and cultivate our own rituals of sounds, smells, words and movements with which we usher ourselves into our awareness of God's presence. On Sunday mornings there might even be bells, but probably larger than the ones in Pavlov's laboratory, and certainly without his cruelty.

 Something to chew as your dog walks alongside you
Can I identify anything that prompts me to turn to God?

PART 8

GOD, DOGS AND US

45

IMAGO DEI AND IMAGO HUMANITATIS (IN THE IMAGE OF GOD AND IN THE IMAGE OF HUMANS)

Just rustle a treat bag and you will witness a major difference between dogs and wolves. Your dog's face will light up. This is our doing. Wolves can't raise their eyebrows in the way our dogs can. And this is entirely a result of our interventions.

At some point in the last 15,000 years, as the Wolf Pact was still being negotiated, a genetic aberration in certain wolves caused a few internal fibres to form a new muscle above the eye. Their pups were born with movable eyebrows and therefore had more expressive faces. They looked more human. Their wider eyes tugged our heartstrings and so we gave them better food and more attention (Disney knows we love big eyes). We controlled their breeding until the aberration became established as the new normal. We thus created a species for ourselves - made in our own image, in 'imago humanitatis', at least in terms of facial expression.

There is food for thought here as we turn to God's relationship with humans. The Bible begins with a description of how human beings were created by God, in God's own image.[60] Since this was first written, much more ink has been spilt as to what 'imago Dei' might mean. Some see it in terms of purpose: we are unique among animals in that we were designed specifically to be God's companions. St Augustine's prayer captures this: 'You have made us for Yourself, O Lord, and our heart is restless until it rests in You.' Others think that being created in 'imago Dei' makes us superior to the rest of creation, which either legitimises our right to exploit or appoints us as stewards: two trains of thought heading to two very different destinations. A cynic might add that all these are exactly the sort of claims that the first creature capable of speech would make for themselves ... and then fortify, by enshrining in holy text.

There is a fun additional argument, that can run concurrently, namely that dogs tamed us just as much as we tamed them. Their aid and influence civilised us into the kind of species that could provide for their needs. The humans who possessed dog-friendly genes thrived and passed their DNA on to subsequent generations. There were others who eschewed dogs, but nevertheless survived alongside the dog-loving. This might explain how humanity is now so divided: the genetically dog-friendly spend billions on toys, treats, insurance and vet bills, while some of those lacking this bias, treat dogs as disposable, seemingly unmoved by canine suffering. If you have stayed thus far with this book, it is likely that you belong with me, in the first group. We have inherited from those who felt incomplete without dogs. And if we value our dogs' companionship, how much more does God values ours?

Our ancestors exploited a chance mutation, which led our them to breed friendly wolves into 'imago humanitatis', i.e. dogs. But if St Augustine is correct, imago Dei means that God did not rely on luck, but deliberately made us with a clear desire for our companionship now in this life, and forever in eternity.

[60] Genesis 1:27.

Something to chew as your dog walks alongside you
Can it be true that God made me for companionship and values my company?

46

IMAGO DOG

Maybe we should not be too hard on ourselves if at times we fall into the trap of anthropomorphism, by which I mean imagining our dogs to be almost human. After all, they do a very similar thing with us. Apparently your dog regards you less as a human, a member of a separate species and more as some kind of weird bipedal dog. They stretch the bounds of their self-image to accommodate us, re-casting us in *imago dog*. And they do this despite our bizarrely non-canine behaviour.

If anthropomorphism is the attributing of human characteristics to non-humans, what word would describe dogs regarding non-dogs as canine-ish? I tried swapping the Greek for human (*anthropos*) for the Greek for dog (*skýlos*) and concocted 'skylomorphism'. Google does not seem to like this much and to be fair, it hardly trips off the tongue. Much could be explained however if skylomorphism really is a thing; for instance why do our dogs become upset or confused when they see us, their fellow 'dogs' excluding them? We feast and tell them to lie down away from us. We snack continually but restrict their eating to set meal times. We abandon them, locking them alone in the den while we go out on adventures, presumably hunting for food or exploring new territory. We sleep on beds, sometimes in pairs, but consign them to a lonely basket. We hardly ever sniff things and even more bizarrely, we get irrationally ratty when they take an interest in our more aromatic areas. If to our dogs, we are also dogs, then our behaviour towards them, is surely mysterious and at times, might even seem cruel.

As humans, we do not merely anthropomorphise 'downwards' (by imagining our dogs as humans, only a little less so) we also anthropomorphise upwards, imagining God to be pretty much the same as us, only a bit wiser and a bit more powerful. We can misuse '*qal wahomer*'. The principle does not work in every case. We cannot always reason, 'If I think something, then God probably thinks pretty much the same, only more so.' Such misuse can be disastrous. Have you ever wondered why some religious people are so miserable, self-righteous and unloving, despite the many hours they spend in prayer? Or why so much violence is done by supposedly religious people - from all faiths. The answer might be this simple: their god is not God, but rather a flimsy ramped-up version of themselves, who exists unchallenged, solely to reassure them that they are always right.

This is one of the reasons why fellowship with other believers is so important: our images of God, false, true, immature, seasoned and all variants in between, are confronted each time we encounter someone who sees God differently. Christianity teaches that God has become one of us and one with us but that does not make God exactly the same as me or you and certainly not by any extension, me the same as God. The prophet Isaiah once heard God saying:

> For my thoughts are not your thoughts,
> nor are your ways my ways,
> says the Lord.
> For as the heavens are higher than the earth,
> so are my ways higher than your ways
> and my thoughts than your thoughts.[61]

---

[61]   Isaiah 55:8-9.

If God was no more than a super-wise, extra-loving version of you or me, then God's behaviour might seem bizarre, at times even cruel. But if we can grasp that we are different from dogs … and that God is even more so from us, then we might see God as both mysterious *and* worthy of our trust.

Something to chew as your dog walks alongside you
How might I become aware that I am carrying false images of God?

SO NOTHING POSITIVE AOUT US AS DOGS THEN?

WELL... NOT REALLY, BUT MAYBE...

47

DOGS IN THE BIBLE

It is a sad fact, that the scribes who wrote the Bible did not see dogs as we do. Dogs were around, as they are in all human societies. They had some value as guards, but this was tempered by the fear of rabies. Their scavenging was also off-putting. When the dreadful Queen Jezebel died, her ignominy was compounded by the denial of a proper burial. Her body was disposed of in the worst way imaginable to her contemporaries. It was eaten by dogs.

This is just one example of how dogs do not do well in the Bible. It is hard to find many affirming references. They are either, like fools returning to their own vomit[62] or competing with prostitutes for a dead king's blood.[63] Calling someone 'a dead dog' was quite the go-to insult in Old Testament times. In the gospels, dogs might appear under the table to eat fallen crumbs, but only in a gentile home.[64]

Biblical studies has a technical term, 'synonymous parallelism'. This is where a single concept is reinforced by being stated twice over two lines and in two different ways. The psalmist saw danger in both swords and dogs:

[62]   Proverbs 26:11.
[63]   1 Kings 22:37.
[64]   Mark 7:24-29.

'Deliver my soul from the sword, my life from the power of the dog!'[65]

Jesus (sadly, in my opinion) lumped dogs and pigs together, as unworthy of holy treats:

'Do not give what is holy to dogs; and do not throw your pearls before swine.'[66]

Quite what any Bible character would make of our pampered pooches, who live inside our homes and sometimes sleep in our beds, I can only guess. My hopes are not high. Dogs just did not have the status there and then, that they enjoy here and now. If we hold the Bible in a particular light, we might find a few pro-dog passages, but these are very slim pickings:

- Prior to the Exodus, when all Egypt was shaking with loud laments at the deaths of their firstborn, the Hebrews were left in peace. We read that not even a dog barked at them.[67] Some believe that a later command to give all carrion to dogs was a reward for their silence on that night.[68]
- Psalm 145:9 is a welcome catch all, explaining how God's goodness and compassion is for all creation, and therefore for dogs too: 'The Lord is good to all; he has compassion on all he has made.'
- In the apocryphal Book of Tobit, Raphael has a dog who seems to serve no other purpose than as the angel's welcome companion.[69]
- In one of Jesus' parables, the poor man Lazarus received nothing from the rich man, at whose gates he lay, but the local dogs

---

[65] Psalm 22:20.
[66] Matthew 7:6 This is surely a verse to confound any Christian dog owners who insist on a rigid, fundamentalist approach to the Scriptures.
[67] Exodus 11:7.
[68] Exodus 22:31.
[69] Tobit 6:2 and 11:4.

licked his wounds.[70] This might be a sign, either of his utter degradation *or* of a smidgeon of kindness. Dog saliva contains various antibacterial enzymes, which might have benefitted Lazarus. I recognise that naming this a pro-dog story might be pushing my pro-dog agenda a step too far, but since no humans had stepped forward to deliver divine compassion to Lazarus, maybe God delegated this task to dogs.

But even if the Bible had nothing good to say about dogs, we cannot conclude that God does not value them. In this case, the Bible's record is more a reflection on the societies of the time, than on God. Sparrows likewise do not receive a good press, they are cheap and apparently their poo can cause blindness,[71] but as mentioned before, not a single one falls to the ground unnoticed by God.[72]

Something to chew as your dog walks alongside you
If I could whisper into one of the ancient psalmists' ears, what kind words would I wish to say about dogs?

---

[70] Luke 16:19-31.
[71] Tobit 2:10.
[72] Matthew 10:29.

48

MORE FROM THE BIBLE – PETS AND PLAYTIME

The prophet Nathan goads King David to score a goal and then revel in the anticipation of applause. Nathan then reveals to him that he was facing the wrong way, thus making his goal an own goal, the kind of own goal which should probably see him disqualified from the team.[73] Stay with me, this will get around to dogs, eventually.

It all started when David got the hots for a woman called Bathsheba. This is despite him having more than enough wives and concubines already. He has Bathsheba bought to his palace where he has sex with her. We are told nothing from Bathsheba's point of view. This might have been a fully consensual coupling or perhaps Bathsheba was presented with the kind of 'options' Harvey Weinstein so often issued to the women in his power? I imagine it would have been hard to say, 'No' to a king, such as David. Once Bathsheba has fallen pregnant, David recalls Uriah, her soldier husband from the wars and tries to coerce him into sleeping with her and when he does not, David has him killed.

The prophet Nathan approaches David asking for his judgement

[73]   2 Samuel 12:1-12.

in a case of injustice. A poor man had a lamb, who was his pet. The lamb was like a daughter to him, sharing cup and cuddles. His rich neighbour needed to entertain a guest and although he had more than enough sheep of his own *(how did David not see this trap as it was being set?)* he stole the poor man's pet, killed it, cooked it and served it up. On hearing this, David becomes so hopping mad at this pitiless act, that he pronounces death to the rich man. At this moment Nathan reveals the own goal David has just scored.

Dogs may not get a very good press in the Scriptures, but the concept of pets is clearly not alien. Cats get no mention at all. But neither Nathan nor David question why a poor man would keep a lamb as a pet. If it was indeed God, who fired up Nathan with courage to challenge David, then can we conclude that God also recognises that pets are family (we read that the ewe was 'as a daughter')? And can we then assume that when the Bible says 'lamb' or 'sheep', we, from our cultural viewpoint might sometimes read 'pet' and maybe even … 'dog'? A parable about a good owner who does not rest until her lost dog is found, makes perfect sense.

There is also a tradition within Judaism which imagines God spending the final quarter of each day, out sporting with Leviathan, very much as we would relax from our work with our pooches and a few rounds of fetch or tug of war.[74] I like the idea of God playing with a favourite pet.

 Something to chew as your dog walks alongside you
What happens when I rework Psalm 23, beginning: 'My Alpha is my owner, I shall not want for anything'?

---

[74] The Talmud in Avodah Zarah 3b says that in the last quarter of the day God plays with the Leviathan. 'During the fourth three hours, He sits and makes sport with the leviathan, as it is stated: "There is leviathan, whom You have formed to sport with" (Psalms 104:26). Evidently, God makes sport every day, not only on that one day.' https:// www.sefaria.org/Avodah_Zarah. 3b.8?lang=en&with=all&lang2=en

A SMALL DOG FINDS
INSPIRATION FROM
SIR JACOB EPSTEIN

49

HOW A SMALL DOG ILLUMINATED A BIBLE STORY

A small dog taught us a Bible story halfway up a Greek mountain. Our plan to admire a sunset, was frustrated by the state of the road. A recent earth tremor had ruptured a large section of it, leaving it more suitable for a four by four than for our little hire car. We parked up, collected our cameras and set out.

On returning to the car, we found a small white dog sitting by one of the front wheels. He seemed friendly enough. He wagged his tail and approached us, with just enough wobble to indicate that he was still a pup. We talked to him and scratched his head and then made ready to leave. But the moment we started the engine, he darted under the car. I jumped out to check he was safe. He was. He had lodged himself into a very dangerous place, right in front of the nearside wheel. I called to him but he refused to come. Eventually I knelt down, picked him up and carried him to the verge. As soon as I'd put him down he ran straight back to his former place. We repeated this exercise several times. I explained to him that he'd get squashed if he stayed there and how we could not take him with us (our accommodation had a strict 'no pets' policy). And still he kept on returning to the same spot, in front of the wheel. His message was clear: 'You can kill me or you can take me with you. But what you can't do is leave me here.'

We tried revving the engine, reversing an inch (to make him aware that cars move) and peeping the horn. His answer was the same: 'Take me or kill me but don't leave me.' This continued for what felt like an age, but was probably only ten minutes. We must have been making quite some noise, because a woman came out from a nearby house to investigate. I did that strange thing we do when we cannot speak a foreign language, which involves pointing and hopeful sounds; I was trying to say: 'Is this your dog?' She answered in a broad Yorkshire accent: 'I've seen it around, but it's not mine.' We explained our problem, how we wanted to move on, but were being held up by this dog. She was a kind person. She picked him up and looked over him. 'You know he's got a sheep tick on him? But I can fix that.' It turned out that she did some volunteering at a local animal shelter and promised to take him there the next day. I took one last look at him. He had snuggled up to her, his long nose lying across the base of her neck. And, maybe it was just how his mouth naturally rested ... or maybe not ... but I could swear that he looked as if he was smiling. He was safe. He had found a new pack, at least for the night.

Back home in our flat in Manchester I often thought about him, wondering what had become of him. I tried to work his story into a Good Samaritan episode, with us in the title role. We had after all, left him in the care of an 'innkeeper'. But there was too much that did not fit. We could hardly claim the Samaritan's enthusiasm. Neither were we Priest or Levite, passing by on the other side, offering no help but at least inflicting no further injury. This dog had not given us such an easy out. For a while our only choice had been to rescue him or squash him. If there was a Good Samaritan, the woman was a far better candidate than either of us.

I then thought of a different passage in the Bible, one which I had never truly understood before. Jacob was out late one night when he met a man and fought with him. They wrestled together until daybreak, neither winning. Then the man, or we should say 'angel' made a decisive move that secured him the victory. Jacob, though defeated, still clung to him, saying, 'I will not let you go, unless you bless me.'[75] So the angel blessed him and then went away.

This little white dog likewise refused to be dismissed without the blessing he needed. He seemed so certain that he belonged and needed to belong. Had we been able to adopt him, choosing his name would not have been hard.

Something to chew as your dog walks alongside you
Could I have the same conviction as Jacob (both the man and the little white dog): that I matter, that I have value, that I *will* be blessed, no matter what the struggle?

---

[75] Genesis 32:26.

YEH! AND IT'S US WHO ARE
THE DANGEROUS SAVAGES!

50

SALVATION

Our childhood dog once got his leg caught in an illegal snare, no doubt intended for rabbits. I was not there. My mother told me the story. The family friend who was walking him, at once fell to his knees and started fumbling to open the trap. The dog, in pain and panic bit deep into his arm. The dog was not to blame for this. He did not understand. His mind was completely overrun by sudden and inexplicable shock.

The memory of this story returned to me years later, as my husband and I were walking along a country lane in Greece. A burst of violent shuddering drew our attention down a steep verge to a fence, and to a head protruding through one of its wire squares. It belonged to a small brown and white goat. Its rounded horns had presented no obstacle on the way in, but now they were, as if designed for this very purpose, preventing its withdrawal. It was stuck, well and truly. Its range of movement limited to the length of its neck. There was nothing it could do to save itself. It was caught in too strong a trap. It needed help beyond its own resources. It was frightened. It bucked back and forth, making the racket that had first alerted us. And in full Good Samaritan mode I scrambled down to free it.

This was not easy. It did not cooperate. And why would it? A strange human approaching when it was already vulnerable, surely ramped up its nightmare. My soothing words did nothing to calm it. Remembering the story of our childhood dog, I kept my hands as far as possible from its mouth, while struggling to prise the wire square into the shape that would allow its curling horns to pass back through, but every time I came close to success, the goat lunged backwards or rammed forwards, returning us to stage one. It stretched, squashed, battered and bruised my fingers in its panic. Its rescue could have been accomplished in a matter of moments, had it stayed still, had it trusted me, but it could not. And then suddenly the stars and the planets all aligned and the gap I was straining to create momentarily matched the angle of its horned head. It shot backwards, staggering as if drunk on its newfound freedom.

There are videos of seals freed from discarded fishing nets; they seem to pause and turn as if thanking their human rescuers, before plunging back into the sea. My goat did no such thing. It bounded with all its caprine agility deep into the undergrowth, off towards the bells of its herd.

I felt rather pleased with myself. The joy of achievement far outweighing the pain in my fingers. Later on, as I reflected on the difficulty of saving another creature from danger, I turned the tables and tried to imagine God's perspective. If saving one goat had been hard work for me, how infinitely more so was Christ's struggle to redeem unwilling, uncooperative, confused, distressed and at times, ungrateful humans from the snare we had fallen into? And I glimpsed afresh how there was nothing straightforward or painless about that mysterious operation.

 Something to chew as your dog walks alongside you
How often do I 'survey the wondrous cross'? And where do such reflections leave me?

IT'S GREAT... BUT I HAVE
SOME QUESTIONS

51

REUNIONS IN HEAVEN?

In 2014 there was flurry of excitement as a rumour spread. Apparently Pope Francis had declared that we will see our animals again in heaven. The story told how he had been overheard one rainy afternoon, in St Peter's Square comforting a small boy, distraught at the death his dog. His reported words were, 'Paradise is open to all of God's creatures.' Dog lovers around the world rejoiced at this papal confirmation of what they had always more than suspected. The problem was, he did not say this. The quotation belongs to Pope Paul VI who died in 1978. The story began 'The Pope said …' without mentioning which Pope. Nevertheless the media allowed it to run, watching it tango with the popularity of the new Pontiff, who had taken his new name from the patron saint of animals.

For a great many dog owners there is no scrap of doubt that we will meet our dogs again. Hence the popularity of the film, *All Dogs Go To Heaven*, which spawned a sequel, a TV series and a Christmas Special. Many other films involving the afterlife, such as Tim Burton's *Corpse Bride*, tell stories about dogs being reunited with their owners. We talk of the rainbow bridge. Our dogs wait for us in a lush green meadow, we meet them there when we die, and together cross over into heaven, never to be separated again.

This is the kind of comfort for which we fumble in grief, when we cannot countenance our dog being gone forever. But neither desperation nor earnest wishes can ever stand as substitute for divine revelation. The truth is, we do not know much about what will happen beyond death. The Bible offers us no reassurances about our dogs, but there again, why would it? Such thoughts would never have occurred to the dog-disregarding-humans who wrote it. I fervently hope there will be joyful reunions. But then I drown in a slew of unanswerable questions about the eternal fate of other animals, including those we have eaten, worn or driven to extinction. Have they also gone to heaven? Or is paradise open only to humans and our pets?

This whole narrative about us 'dying and going to heaven' needs to be questioned. Bishop and biblical scholar N. T. Wright speaks about the coming era when renewed heaven and renewed Earth unite to become a new creation, where God dwells with humans forever. I am very much hoping that dogs, as part of the old creation will feature in the new. But I still hanker for a deeper wish. I want more than eternity with dogs, I want to meet my own dogs again (although how they will all get on with each other is another worry).

Following the death of one very dear dog and scrabbling to clutch at any straw, I came across a rather hard to interpret line in St Paul's First Letter to the Corinthians.[76] He speaks of an unbelieving spouse, being granted salvation because of their binding relationship with a believer and their membership of a believing household. I decided to hope that maybe my love for my dog, might contain something of the same salvific power and thus bring about our eventual reunion. Admittedly this is all rather flimsy, but the Bible did not give me much to work with. Over time, I found I could leave such unanswerable questions with God, as I do my other queries about what happens next. (And since I have watched the TV series *The Good Place*, I have plenty of fresh ones.)

In the meantime, we find there are a great many dogs here with us now, who are less interested in heaven and more in finding

[76] I Corinthians 7:14.

some decent treatment here on Earth. And so as grief loses its raw bite and when we are ready, we should devote our energies less to speculations about departed dogs and more to the welfare of current dogs.

Something to chew as your dog walks alongside you
How do I feel when contemplating eternity? Hopeful? Anxious? Elated? Or more confused than anything else?

'HADDIE'

52
HADDIE'S PSALM

Haddie is a beautiful dog, scarred by human cruelty.[77] She was a bait dog. If you don't want to know what a bait dog is, skip the next paragraph, which is upsetting.

A bait dog has one function only. Certain degraded humans use it as a disposable item to train their fighting dogs to kill. They take a living dog, sometimes taping its mouth shut and then throw it to their already aggressive dogs. The bait dogs that survive, might later be killed or just simply abandoned. The terrible irony is that the perverted humans who treat a pup as bait, must have some feeling for dogs: they keep, feed and care for their brutalised fighters. This, along with eating dogs is an utter betrayal of the Wolf Pact. True humanity surely baulks in sickened revulsion at any kind of 'enjoyment' which is dependent on another creature's misery.

[77] You can follow her on Instagram @haddiethepiratedog.

HADDIE'S PSALM

Haddie was once a bait dog. Her injuries were appalling, but now they somehow make her innocent sweetness shine all the more brightly. She was rescued. And then she was adopted by Erin, who has given me permission to share her story. They are now together in Washington DC where Haddie lives a wonderful dog life. Taking my cue from a previous reading, I have imagined Haddie's version of Psalm 23:

> My Alpha is my owner,
> I shall not want for anything.
> She provides snug spaces where I can sleep safely.
> She leads me to parks bursting with exciting smells.
> When I was being tormented, she found me and took me in.
> She keeps me safe with collar, lead, ID chip and bandana.
> She posts pictures and videos of me online,
> And those who once hurt me, can now see my value.
> She gives me medicines and cuddles,
> And my heart is full to overflowing.
> She has promised that my future with her is non-negotiable;
> her home, is my home and shall be all the days of my life.

Can dogs forgive? Each time Haddie appears on my screen I am amazed at her trusting nature. She wags her tail so hard, it often appears as a blur. She plays with other dogs. She loves her humans. She calls to my mind the phrase, 'forgiveness is giving up the hope of a better past'. By this definition, Haddie has forgiven. With the love of Erin and of those who first rescued her, she seems to have put her awful past behind her. Her former persecutors

have no place or purchase in her thoughts. She has made her life a testimony less to human cruelty and more to the power of love. And if this is so with Haddie and Erin, how much more so can this be with us and God?

Something to chew as your dog walks alongside you
When I feel sickened by human cruelty, what action do I take? And out of all the definitions of forgiveness, how do I rate, 'giving up the hope of a better past'?

CONCLUSION
'...AND THE GREATEST IS LOVE'

And at the end of all this, a question remains; a question that many dog owners ponder, 'But does she *love* me?' or 'Does he see me as anything more than his feeder/provider?' Are dogs capable of love or do they merely display a series of pre-programmed, inherited instincts that aid their survival in a pack, up to and, hopefully beyond, the point where they have successfully passed on their DNA? When they cuddle up to us, are they expressing affection or are they just seeking some shared body heat?

It raises that most profound question, 'What is love?' And if that does not plant an earworm into your skull, nothing will. Pop song lyricists, together with philosophers and even princes have long contemplated exactly what being 'in love' means.

Do dogs love? They trust us. They seek our company. They miss us when we go. They rejoice at our return. They defer certain canine instincts in obedience to us. They prefer us over other animals. They become jealous if we give too much attention to another dog. They give us prolonged eye contact. They are patient with us. They forgive with us. Should the need arise, they defend us. They share their toys

157

with us. They love our smells, even those we're less keen about. It's not a bad record. It sounds a lot like love, more than 'close enough', more than just 'puppy love'.

We humans could set ourselves the same examination. Do we love? Do we love each other? Can we say that we truly love God, or do we merely exhibit a range of learnt and instinctive behaviours so we can pass on our DNA, prosper in this life and hopefully enter the next? What is love? We'll keep on asking.

I strongly suspect God rejoices in all our human and canine expressions of love, however flawed, fickle or fallible. God knows of what we are made, and yet loves us. God is love, and we only love because God first loved us.[78]

So yes, in my book (quite literally) our dogs *are* capable of love and they *do* love us. And their love for us, along with our love for them, offers us rich hints of the wonders of God's love.

How should we love God? How should we love our dogs? And how much further can I push the line, 'if something is so with us and our dogs, *how much more so* is it with God and us'? I began this short book intending a light-hearted series of paddlings and splashings about, but as I progressed I found myself wading into ever deeper waters. I should not be surprised: questions about God and dogs penetrate all the way to the human core.

Here's the prophet Micah, with a way forward:

'He has told you, O mortal, what is good; and what does the Lord require of you but to do justice, and to love kindness, and to walk humbly with your God?'[79]

This seems as good a guide to loving God as any, for us dog walkers and for our dogs, so that together we can enjoy our 'walkies' with God and our place on God's sofa.

[78]   1 John 4:10.
[79]   Micah 6:8.

ACKNOWLEDGEMENTS

This book belongs first and foremost to my husband Haydn, who loves me enough to embrace my crazed need for canine companionship.

Many others have helped me as I have written. I have been inspired by Mac Grannan, Nico and Gypsy Fogg, Chewie Calladine, Ayla and Truffs Stretton, Flynn Crosbee, Nelly Pitt, Mimi and Tosca El Safany, Eric Painter, Haddie (the pirate dog), Duke Ford, Jarvis Lucas, Sam de Weimar and Alfie Day.

After fruitlessly racking my brains to retrieve the words 'qal wahomer' (last encountered over a quarter of a century ago) the Reverend Dr Ian Wallis came to my rescue. Rabbi Jonathan Wittenberg kindly responded to my questions, helping me with certain Scriptural references. Anne El Safany and Guy Elsmore have generously gone through the entire script making invaluable suggestions. I remain ever grateful to David Moloney and all the team at DLT for their continuing support and encouragement. I stand in awe of the volunteers and workers, especially at Mornac SPA and Association En Route, who work so hard to rescue dogs from danger and find them loving homes.

I have attempted (and I cannot judge how successfully) to make this a book about *all* dogs, rather than just *our* dogs: Hugo and Hera our two Beaubradors[80]. My walks with Hugo gave me the impetus to start jotting down my God-humans-and-dogs-thoughts. Hera appeared in the late-editing stage, long after the

---

[80] 'Beaubrador' is my name for Beauceron-Labrador cross, which is not an official or recognised breed (and I remain convinced that the best possible, the most desirable breed, is always a Rescue).

text had been completed, but cannot go unmentioned. While writing, I enjoyed wonderful memories of two other Labrador crosses, Nelson (our childhood dog) and Talisker (the one and only). I miss them both and am so glad that we shared each other's lives.